TESTIMONY

EXCHANGING OUR FORMER SEXUAL IDENTITY FOR OUR NEW IDENTITY IN CHRIST

JAMES RONDINONE

JAMES **RONDINONE**
PUBLICATIONS

Unless otherwise indicated, Scripture quotations are taken from the King James Version (KJV)-public domain.

Printed in the United States of America.

Paperback ISBN-13: 9798499921913

CONTENTS

Introduction v

Chapter 1 1
Why do we Come to Jesus?

Chapter 2 7
Being Active in Church Activities Doesn't Necessarily Mean We Are Growing Spiritually

Chapter 3 15
Do You Know How God Sees You? Do You Know Who You Are in Christ?

Chapter 4 24
What Is God's Will or Plan for My Life?

Chapter 5 30
What Does It Mean to Love One Another with God's Love?

Chapter 6 42
Should a Christian Follow Societal Norms Concerning Sexual Behavior?

Chapter 7 51
What Should Determine the Way a Believer Should Think, Speak, and Act?

Chapter 8 68
God Made Me Like This

Chapter 9 76
How Do Christians Learn to No Longer Be in Subjection to the Cravings and Desires of Their Flesh?

Chapter 10 82
How Do We Cultivate the Spiritual Grace Called Temperance So That We Will Became An Overcomer in the Area of Eros Sexual Desires?

Chapter 11 97
Testimonies about Maintaining Continual Victory over Sexual Abuse and Sinful Sexual Desires

Epilogue 123

Endnotes 127

INTRODUCTION

I'm writing this study to help fellow believers who are having difficulty walking with God, especially in addressing their sexual inclinations or propensities. This study came about as my wife and I were watching the news on TV, and a story about sexual abuse in a particular mainstream church was being reported. The allegation was that many, who were leaders in the church, preyed upon young boys and forced them to have sexual relations. Not only were these actions reprehensible, but something else we were told was even more shocking. There were some in leadership who were aware of these liaisons but did not report them as criminal actions to the civil authorities. In fact, they did all they could to keep quiet whatever happened, along with eventually relocating these sexual predators to resume their position in the church somewhere else.

A few days later, my wife found an article on the internet involving sexual misconduct that had to do with a well-known Christian megachurch. I was familiar with this church mainly because of its Christian music, which I listen to almost daily. So, she sent the article to my email, and I proceeded to read it. The name of the article is entitled, *Sex Abuse & Gay Conversion Therapy: The Dark Past of Justin Bieber's Megachurch Hillsong.*[1]

What resonated with me were a few things. The founder of the original ministry, which was initially under a different name, allegedly admitted to abusing some of the young boys in the church. Eventually, he resigned. His son took over the ministry under a new name. As I continued to read the article, something else caught my attention, and that was how there were some members and/or former members, who were not happy with the church's stance on gay marriage, gays in leadership, and in general, how they were being treated.

Some of their comments set my mind in motion. I wanted to help them in the perception of their walk with God. One of their comments was, "I can't worship at a church knowing that [I'm] not fully accepted and considered equal to all those around me."[2] Another one was, "... surrounded by people that might love me as a person but [don't] accept me as being gay; instead, tolerate me."[3] The final one was, "...people who don't recognize that any relationship that I have with a man is part of God's plan and that it would be full of love, equal to any other."[4]

Certain sections of the article have been omitted so that the three comments mentioned are what is focused upon. I included the article so that you could be aware of the context in which these perceptions were conveyed.

SEX ABUSE & GAY CONVERSION THERAPY: THE DARK PAST OF JUSTIN BIEBER'S MEGACHURCH HILLSONG

... The forerunner to Hillsong was founded in 1977 by Australian pastor Frank Houston, who created the Sydney Christian Life Centre. Frank's son—current Hillsong lead pastor Brian Houston—and Brian's wife, Bobbie (also a pastor), worked there under Frank until [1983] when the couple left to start their own church. They called it Hills Christian Life Centre, named for the suburbs of Sydney in New South Wales where it was located. They started with just [forty-five] congregants; today, Hillsong churches operate in [fourteen] countries and claim to welcome some [one hundred thousand] worshippers every week. They believe that Jesus Saves and the Bible should be read literally—and that worship should be an experience: singing and clapping, speaking in tongues, faith healing.

In 1999, when Frank retired—or was fired, depending on your semantic druthers—Brian merged his father's church with his own, and rebranded under the name Hillsong, after his in-house music ministry that was quickly winning fans worldwide. Hillsong's biggest draw has always been the music: Some [forty] albums and hundreds of songs have been produced under the church's umbrella since 1992, raking in millions. …

[This] brings us to what Brian Houston calls "the elephant in the room," or "the gay situation."

When Alex Pittaway's youth pastor stood before a group of 800 evangelical Christian boys and men in Sydney and shouted, "Shirts off!" everybody listened. Boys as young as [thirteen] and their leaders, some as old as 30, all ripped off shirts in a sign of godly macho solidarity. Someone jumped on stage and was shouted down, with jeers of "Go to the gym, mate!"

It wasn't just pastor Scott "Sanga" Samways (the nickname is slang in Australia for a sausage sandwich) who utilized partial nudity as a church-approved bonding technique, Pittaway said. At youth group and Bible camp, or any time when men and women were separated, Alex remembers "a hell of a lot of homoerotic [behavior]."

For Alex—a closeted gay teen and member of Hillsong—the command was terrifying. Did the brothers in Christ slapping his back or complimenting his abs know he was gay? If someone knew, would he think Alex was "looking"?

Alex quit the church in [2008] after a traumatic coming out where he says he was referred by his youth pastor to counseling that proposed to make him straight—the kind of conversion therapy we now know is based on pseudoscience, as ineffectual as [it's] damaging.

For years, in fact, coming out to a Hillsong pastor landed a church member in just such an 'ex-gay' program. According to former members, Hillsong first helped congregants struggling with their sexuality pray their gay away in Exit Ministries, started by Frank Houston, or Mercy Ministries for lesbians; the church then outsourced the conversion work to Living Waters (self-shuttered in 2014) or Exodus ([/content/dailybeast/articles/2013/06/21/exodus-closes-marking-official-end-of-the-ex-gay-movement.html] closed in 2013), or maybe an online course like Setting Captives Free (banned in the Apple Store in 2013). Self-proclaimed reformed [gay] and former executive director of Exodus, Sy Rogers—who now identifies as transgender and is married to a woman—wrote books and tapes and would preach at Hillsong conferences about overcoming his gay demons. He'd tell the struggling faithful: "You gotta learn to bow down and obey and deal with it." Rogers's current ministry has moved away from the ex-gay [message,] and though Rogers hasn't said so publicly, Brian Houston told a blogger that Rogers probably regrets his involvement with Exodus.

But Hillsong doesn't try to "fix" gay congregants anymore. Sometime around 2011, Houston distanced his church from conversion programs, and he now talks often about the "weight" the church bears when it comes to its treatment of gays and lesbians. "They feel like 'maybe I'm gay' and they go to a youth leader and they are rejected," Brian said in a 2013 sermon. "At that [moment,] a great hatred comes in. At that moment some of them have gone so far with the rejection and gone to parents who didn't understand and ended up committing suicide. That's the weight we live with."

It should be said here that Alex, now an openly gay seminary student in Indiana, still thinks of Hillsong fondly, speaks of it warmly, and often catches himself humming the church tunes. He says that while he didn't feel safe or comfortable trying to find God in a building where most of the people in it thought he was going to hell, for those who don't define themselves by their sexuality, who can compartmentalize, it's a fine place to "worship anonymously."

Ben Fenlon, a three-year member of Hillsong's London satellite, explained his reasons for quitting the church in a piece for the Huffington Post. He wrote, "I can't worship at a church knowing that [I'm] not fully accepted and considered equal to all those around me.

Surrounded by people that might love me as a person but [don't] accept me as being gay; [instead,] tolerate me. People who might tell me that being gay is okay, but on the inside are praying for me to let Jesus move in my life and change me. People who don't recognize that any relationship that I have with a man is part of God's plan and that it would be full of love, equal to any other."

Alex told me about a gay friend who had been booted from his position in Hillsong's children's ministry after he came out and another who, after coming out to Hillsong leadership, was relieved of his duties as an usher. "He wasn't even allowed to serve cups of coffee or help direct traffic in the parking lot," he said. (Hillsong did not return requests for comment on these alleged incidents.)

"Gay people need to know that when they go to Hillsong, they have to go to the back of the bus." Alex said. "Hillsong is hip and attractive and contemporary, but there's certainly nothing contemporary about what LGBT people will face if they want to be a leader in the church or offer themselves up for service. That's something [Hillsong] will have to be upfront with, and they haven't been so far."

To be fair, Hillsong's task isn't an easy one. How does an extremely conservative [Pentecostal] church fight irrelevancy and attract those coveted millennials—a group that's been running from churches and overwhelmingly supports gay marriage and equal rights for LGBT people—and maintain its tithing, if intolerant, base at the same time?

Hillsong has taken certain halting steps that place the church to the left of its conservative counterparts, some of which have labeled the Aussie megachurch as [unbiblical] and say its leaders have sold out God's word for a younger, more tolerant crowd. For [example] Hillsong Leadership College recently removed homosexuality from the list of "sexual sins" in the student code of conduct. And some members have taken Pastor Carl Lentz's stance—[basically,] that homosexuality is a sin, [okay], but no worse than any other, and he gets why everyone is always asking, but he'd rather not address it, because Jesus pretty much didn't, and Hillsong loves everyone anyway —as a move in the right direction.

It's not just conservative churches that are criticizing Hillsong's stance. Anna Flowers, pastor at Greenpoint Reformed Church in Brooklyn—a "progressive, young and vibrant church" where she shares the pulpit with two lesbian pastors and one transgender male pastor—has tweeted about what she calls Hillsong's false permissiveness. "not as hip as Hillsong Hipsters, but we actually love and accept everyone," she said in one tweet. In another: "drives us NUTS when Hipster [evangelical] churches fool [people] into thinking they are progressive." Flowers tells me, "[There] are far more truly progressive churches than people realize. And sometimes churches look more progressive than they really are."

I read as many of Lentz's statements on the LGBT issue as I could [find,] and he gave what I consider the most straightforward answer to Jonathan Merritt at Religion News Service in August of 2015 (emphasis mine):

"Our beliefs on biblical marriage and sexual morality *have never changed* at Hillsong church. Yet we stay open and desperate in our pursuit of the [whosoever's]."

What that means in practical terms is that Hillsong wants anyone and everyone in the [seats] but neither supports same-sex marriage nor allows LGBT people to serve in positions of leadership. As Brian Houston clarified last year, following the sacking of a choir director who announced his same-sex engagement to another member of the choir, acceptance of gays and lesbians extends only as far {the pew}.

And for some, including Josh Canfield and Reed Kelly, the couple at the center of the choir controversy, that's enough. For [now,] at least.

Ben Gresham also still attends Hillsong in Sydney, despite a complicated past with the church, because he believes gay and lesbian members are key to helping the church move forward. "I try and speak to church pastors and leaders when I can and have had some encouraging discussions," he said.

Gresham has told the story of coming out at Hillsong on his blog. After three years of ex-gay therapy, constant praying, even undergoing an exorcism, he realized he would never be straight. The thought of never being able to enter the kingdom of heaven, to marry a woman, to be the person Hillsong told him that God wanted him to be, led him to cut himself with a razor blade, and one night, to drive his speeding car nearly off the side of a highway. He considers the last-minute change of heart a miracle.

"For me, Hillsong still feels like home. It has been a source of harm for me in the past but continues to bring me much joy and help me grow in my faith, which is invaluable," he said. "As a gay man and a [Christian,] I would love to see Hillsong fully affirm and include its queer members. I hope it happens sooner rather than [later,] but given my [experience,] I remain doubtful.

"Hillsong is a big [church,] and so it takes time to move it forward. I just wish they would move a bit faster."[5] ...

What was being conveyed seemed to be saying to me that answers to these comments needed to be addressed. So, let's see if we can find a biblical perspective on each of these concerns. But before I attempt to do this, I would like to present my testimony. The purpose of this is to personally identify with those believers who are having a difficult time in their walk with God. Along with this, it's presented in order to provide clarity as to how we can walk victoriously in Christ irrespective of the sexual inclinations or tendencies that try to distract us every day.

1

WHY DO WE COME TO JESUS?

I'm sure if we were to ask different Christians why they came to Jesus, the answers would be varied and innumerable. Rather than speculate, let me share my testimony with you. In my younger years, I was brought up in a particular church that my parents and their parents were faithful to attend. I can honestly say that I didn't enjoy going to church. I went through all of the different requisites as a young man in this faith but had no appreciation for it.

As we tended to move around a lot due to my father's varied jobs, not only would we find a new place to live but a different church structure that was affiliated with the same mainstream faith. I remember there was one church facility that had a cafeteria in the basement to which attendees could go before service. One of the items they sold was fresh bulky buttered rolls that were out of this world. So, when my father would ask my mother and me if we wanted to go to church, I would respond, yes, if I could get a bulky roll.

One of the drawbacks of moving around a lot was not being able to stay in contact with young males or females with whom I had become friends. When I reached my teenage years, there was a lot of soul searching going on due to many factors. One of the decisions I made was to stop going to church, as I thought of it as a waste of time.

My dad, who was working in a factory, decided to quit and open up his own spa and grill business in town. To my dismay, he demanded I work for him after school. Initially, I looked forward to it but soon found out how difficult it was to work for family. I didn't like the idea of cooking food and waiting on others and eventually expressed my sentiment to my dad that I didn't want to work there anymore. This created a clash between us, which caused a lot of friction. At work, when we labored together, this denigrated to condescending comments projected by my father toward me whenever I made some kind of mistake like over-cooking a burger, too much syrup in a milkshake, etc. Over time, this continual verbal assault caused me to want to leave home as soon as I was of age.

When I became a senior in high school, I started to hang around with the wrong crowd. I got involved with smoking cigarettes, smoking marijuana, and girl-seeking. Following high school, I decided to attend a four-year college and subsequently graduated with a B.S. Degree in Mathematics. I tried persistently to get a high school teaching job in mathematics but to no avail. It seemed like nothing was working out for me. I had no job, no girlfriend, didn't get along with my father, drank heavily, smoked marijuana, and got to a point where I just didn't like myself. I needed a life change.

A few more years went by, and I decided I needed to go back to church. The catalyst for this decision was not only a personal desire to change, but it also had to do with a course I took during my senior year in college. This course was an elective class on the life of King Saul. The professor believed that a description of different events about him was not only contained in different Old Testament books, but he alleged there were errors in the accounts, which in his mind meant that the Bible stories were not true. In other words, this book was errant and not to be believed.

What resonated with me was the fact that God (Jehovah) interacted with King Saul in a personal way. My thought was if He interacted with him in this manner, then does He still interact with us today in a similar way? If He does, then where is He to be found? I had no answer to these questions but nonetheless went on a quest to find out. I decided to attend different churches in my home city to see if I could find Him.

Now that I think back on this, it's evident that God knew I was looking for Him, and He, in turn, was looking for me. On one particular day, a Sunday, as I was leaving the morning shift at my dad's store, a parade commemorating a state holiday was heading past on the main street toward the center of the city. After all of it went by, I followed the procession until it arrived at the city's town hall and dispersed. As I was about to walk back to my father's store and pick up my car, I heard a blaring voice broadcasting words over a loudspeaker.

I turned around and saw a crowd of people gathered, so I walked over to where they were to see why. There was a person speaking about Jesus. I had heard about Him before in my younger years in the church I used to attend, having been told that He was one of the members of a Trinity of one God who revealed Himself in three persons, with the other two being called God the Father and God the Holy Spirit. But what they said about Jesus at this time was not what was conveyed to me about Him before. It was different in the sense that if a person acknowledged they were a sinner to God the Father and believed in who Jesus was and what He had accomplished, they would receive another member of the Trinity into their life called the Holy Spirit and thus have a personal encounter with God. This drew my attention. This is called the gospel message, the good news. While I didn't respond to the gospel message at this time, I found out about their upcoming Bible study and attended it the next time it was scheduled.

After a few days had passed, I showed up at the Bible study and noticed that there were quite a few people in attendance. A spread of food was available for all to partake of. After eating, a pastor stood up, opened in prayer, and shared a message. When he was done, he came over to me and presented the gospel, to which I responded. At that moment, I was overwhelmed with God's peace and joy. This immersion of God's presence stayed with me after that for three full days.

I decided to attend this church regularly and realized that the assembly was made up of a mixture of older folks along with young Spirit-filled believers, who would go out street-evangelizing every week. Sadly, a dispute arose over doctrinal differences, and every one of the young evangelizing team left. Being a new Christian, I didn't know what to do, so I stayed in this church for another couple of months.

What I noticed was that a change had taken place as far as God's presence was concerned. Hymns replaced spiritual songs. Messages seemingly were not fresh (anointed). Doctrinal teachings became more emphasized with directives of, we had better do what was being said or else, which just didn't sit right with me.

If you were rich, you were told not to work as much because your material abundance was considered offensive to those who didn't have much. If you had long hair, you were told to cut it because Jesus wouldn't look like that. We were also told that many people weren't going to go to heaven because God didn't choose them. While I might have been a baby as far as learning and understanding doctrine, I thought that these views just weren't right. I left this church and started looking for another while praying to God that He would find the right place for me to attend and call my spiritual home.

As usual, you couldn't make up for what God did next. On a particular day, while I was driving my car heading to go to work for my father, I noticed a young man on the right side of the road flailing one of his arms, directing me to pull my car over. When I did so, I recognized him as being someone I used to hang around with. I asked him how he was doing, and he responded with something like God has changed my life, and I no longer drink alcohol or take drugs. And then he told me about a Bible study he was attending whose pastor was dynamic. I took down the time and place of the study and went the next time they met.

This Bible study was being held in the home of one of the attendees. When I arrived, there were probably about fifteen or twenty people gathered together. The study opened up with prayer, and then a young pastor started playing the guitar and singing. Everyone sang along. Following the music, a message was brought forth with memorized verses of Scripture being spewed out of his mouth like a machine gun. And along with this, God's presence was saturating my soul. God had led me to the place where He wanted me to be.

After about a year had gone by, the attendance at the study had significantly increased, and the young pastor wanted to purchase a facility where the church assembly could meet, along with providing housing for him and for any others who expressed a desire to live there. Finally, two buildings were purchased that were at one time used as a convent for Catholic nuns. At this time, I was asked by this young pastor if I would consider going on staff as an outreach coordinator and live on the property full time, to which I responded yes.

All I can say is that working in this church position and living at this location was amazing. Worship services were held three times a week. Bible classes from an affiliate Bible college were being offered for credit via videotape. Once a week, there was an opportunity to go street witnessing. And if someone had time off, they could leave early in the morning on a particular day and drive to the affiliated Bible college campus, where they could watch a softball game, attend live radio broadcasts, eat lunch in the cafeteria, attend evening worship service, and return home later that day. This was my schedule for about a year and a half before I left to attend Bible college. My new wife, who I met and married in the faith, accompanied me, along with our newborn child.

What I wanted to bring to the attention of those who are having difficulty in their walk with God, especially in the areas of sexual weakness as reflected in the gay therapy article, is that just because someone is on staff and regularly attending to the many activities that their church has to offer doesn't mean that they won't still be having difficulties in this or any area of their sin nature. You might be wondering how this could be if someone were so immersed in God's work.

This brings us to a discussion about the difference between being saved and growing spiritually, which we'll look at next.

2

BEING ACTIVE IN CHURCH ACTIVITIES DOESN'T NECESSARILY MEAN WE ARE GROWING SPIRITUALLY

So, here we're attending to all that our church has to offer. Our schedule is full, but something is amiss. A battle is going on inside of us. We have begun to gain some knowledge about our Christian faith. Depending on where we're going to church will determine the various doctrinal teachings that will be brought forth.

Over time, we might have learned about what Christ has accomplished for us on the cross in that He paid the debt we owed to God the Father for our sin and subsequently forgave it (canceled and removed the debt from the record). Maybe we have learned about the different gifts of the Holy Spirit, about eternal rewards, about eternal security, about the office leadership gifts, about the seven days of creation, about the Mosaic Law, and much more. But again, something is amiss. What could this be?

Let's begin by taking a look at one of the comments that we highlighted in the introduction section of this study, which was taken from the article pertaining to one of the former church members. Here is the comment again. "I can't worship at a church, knowing that [I'm] not fully accepted and considered equal to all those around me."[6]

. . .

This begs the question, what does it mean to be considered equal or accepted in God's assembly?

I assume that the person who said this was referring to how he perceived other believers were treating him concerning his sexual inclinations or propensities. But before we attempt to answer this question, let's begin by answering this one.

What does it actually mean to be considered equal or accepted according to the world's perspective?

I think that this can be answered by taking a closer look at the following verse taken from the book of Romans.

Romans 12:2

> *And be not conformed to this world: but be ye transformed by the renewing of your mind, that ye may prove what is that good, and acceptable, and perfect, will of God.*

The words *be not conformed* according to Koine Greek means that we as believers are not to put on the form, fashion, or appearance of. Of what, of the world? The words *to this world* can mean a few things, to the standards of the world, to the customs of this life, to the sentiments and morals of men, or the prevailing habits, style, and manners of the world. With that said, let's attempt to answer the antithesis question.

But what does it actually mean to be considered equal or accepted scripturally?

Let's start out by going to the book of 2 Corinthians.

2 Corinthians 5:17

Therefore if any man be in Christ, he is a new creature: old things are passed away; behold, all things are become new.

One of the things to be considered equal means is that at salvation, we have become a new creature (a new creation) just like any other person who has become saved.

Please go to the book just before this one, 1 Corinthians.

1 Corinthians 12:11, 18

But all these worketh that one and the selfsame Spirit, dividing to every man severally as he will. But now hath God set the members every one of them in the body, as it hath pleased him.

Another thing of what it means to be equal is that God the Holy Spirit has given to each of us at least one spiritual gift as it has pleased Him. In other words, God chooses for each of us the spiritual endowment that He decides to bless us with. The purpose of the exercise of such use is to edify the body of Christ. While the gifts may differ, each of us is given at least one of them.

The book of Romans is where we'll go next.

Romans 6:2-4

God forbid. How shall we, that are dead to sin, live any longer therein? Know ye not, that so many of us as were baptized into Jesus Christ were baptized into his death? Therefore we are buried with him by baptism into death: that like as Christ was raised up from the dead by the glory of the Father, even so we also should walk in newness of life.

Something else that has happened to each believer at salvation is they have received the indwelling Spirit into their life. At this time, he/she was baptized by Him into Christ, being identified with Him in His death and burial (as He died to sin on the cross, so he/she likewise has died to sin in the sense of being separated from its power). And as He rose from the dead, likewise he/she has become a new creation who can walk in newness of life in the power of His resurrection.

Where we'll go next is the book of Galatians. There's a particular word found there that connotes equality or acceptance among believers.

Galatians 3:26-28

> *For ye are all the children of God by faith in Christ Jesus. For as many of you as have been baptized into Christ have put on Christ. There is neither Jew nor Greek, there is neither bond nor free, there is neither male nor female: for ye are all one in Christ Jesus.*

We're told that there are no longer any national distinctions between Jew or Greek, there are no longer any class distinctions between a slave or freeman, and lastly, there are no longer any gender distinctions between male or female, for all of us are one in Christ. Some might interpret this as saying that there being no gender distinctions between male and female has to do with a person's allowance for choosing someone to have a sexual relationship, whether of the same gender or not.

However, this is not what these verses are about. If you read them in context, the emphasis is on the fact that no matter what ethnicity you are, no matter whether you happen to be a slave or free, no matter whether you are a man or woman, the same grace of adoption or hope of salvation applies to all and that is by faith in Christ Jesus. This is further illustrated by the use of the words *one in Christ Jesus.*

. . .

What does it mean to be one in Christ Jesus?

These words mean to be equally accepted through the Lord Jesus Christ, to be on the same level, and to be entitled to the same privileges in your Christian profession.[7] These words also mean that they are one and the same man or woman in Christ Jesus.[8] This is another way of saying that no person has any advantage or disadvantage in the Kingdom of God, nor any special privilege for salvation.

To further exemplify this idea of oneness, equality, or acceptance, please go to the book of Ephesians.

Ephesians 2:13-14

> *But now in Christ Jesus ye who sometimes were far off are made nigh by the blood of Christ. For he is our peace, who hath made both one, and hath broken down the middle wall of partition between us;*

There used to be those, albeit unbelieving Gentiles, who were far off from being unacquainted with God, but were made near as they were brought into favor with Him through the blood of Christ. Because of this, God the Father has brought about a peace, or a union, between Jew and Gentile, and between those who have responded to the invitation of salvation in His Son in making them one new people forming one church. This is another description of oneness in that it refers to the reconciliation of both Jews and Gentiles, who were at one time separated, but are now made one in Christ worshiping the same God, having the same Savior, depending on the same atonement, and belonging to the same redeemed family.

These are just some of the areas where Christians are one, equal, or accepted with one another in Christ. But did you know that there are other areas in which we're not equal or accepted in Christ? If you noticed, I didn't use the word *one* because this word pertains to salvation.

. . .

What are those areas where we're not equal or accepted?

Let's begin in the book of Ephesians.

Ephesians 4:11

> *And he gave some, apostles; and some, prophets; and some, evangelists; and some, pastors and teachers;*

God the Father has called some Christians, but not all, to an office gift, to a leadership position in the church.

There's something else of which believers are not equal. Please go to the book of 1 Corinthians.

1 Corinthians 3:14-15

> *If any man's work abide which he hath built thereupon, he shall receive a reward. If any man's work shall be burned, he shall suffer loss: but he himself shall be saved; yet so as by fire.*

Some believers will receive more eternal rewards in the eternal state than others.

And what is reflective of the accumulation of eternal rewards is what we'll look at next. This is found in the book of Philippians.

Philippians 2:12-13

> *Wherefore, my beloved, as ye have always obeyed, not as in my presence only, but now much more in my absence, work out your own salvation with fear and trembling. For*

> *it is God which worketh in you both to will and to do of his good pleasure.*

And here's where there's much disparity from one Christian to another, which is as to our walk with God. Each one of us is told to work out or to put into practice what the Holy Spirit has provided for us at salvation, i.e., we're dead to sin's power and are made alive to operate in newness of life. And because of such, we're to carry out our identification with Christ to its ultimate conclusion, Christ-likeness. The salvation spoken here refers to sanctification, victory over [sin,] and the living of a life pleasing to the Lord Jesus.[9] And this can only happen when God the Holy Spirit is enabling us by His divine power operating in our hearts as we subject ourselves to His ministry.

This begs the question, how are we able to operate in the Spirit's power and not be under the influence of sin? While I've not provided you with the answer to this question, what I can tell you is that once we know what the believer's responsibilities in this area are, the realization of these spiritual realities in our lives will be dependent on the choices each of us makes in our free will.

As for the comment made by one of the members of the Christian church, "I can't worship at a church knowing that [I'm] not fully accepted and considered equal to all those around me,"[10] *there's a clear misunderstanding by this person as to what it means to be accepted, equal, or one in the body of Christ.* So, here is a summary of what these words mean.

- *Oneness* means that no matter who you are, whether of a certain ethnicity, gender, or class, each has the same opportunity for salvation. Once we're saved (by repentance to God the Father and belief in Christ), we're accepted by God the Father.
- As far as *being accepted by other believers,* their acceptance of us should be based on God's acceptance of them at salvation.
- In terms of the idea of *being equal to all those believers around us,* we're equal in the sense that each of us has the

indwelling Spirit, who has provided us with additional benefits, one of which is that He has given to each of us at least one spiritual gift.

- And as for *having equal opportunity,* all of us have equal opportunity to grow spiritually, exercise our gifts, and receive eternal rewards.
- There are, however, *areas where there's no equality.* Not every believer receives a calling to leadership. Spiritual growth varies from believer to believer, and as such, so will eternal rewards.
- And the *acceptance of one another* means that if a fellow believer is living in an area of weakness, we don't simply condone it, but we choose to help them in learning how to be an overcomer in that particular area.

With what was just said, let's proceed in taking a look at the second comment that was made by someone in the same church, which was, "I was surrounded by people that might love me as a person but [don't] accept me as being gay; instead tolerate me."[11] Obviously, it's evident that this Christian was upset because his fellow believers did not accept him as being gay.

What this says to me is that this Christian is unaware of who he is in Christ and what God has done for him at salvation. If he knew about who he is in Christ and what God had done for him, he would have a different view of himself and others. And this would have a direct impact on what he would be thinking, what he would be saying, and what actions he would choose to be engaged in.

I will close this chapter by asking this question to this believer or to any believer who is expressing this sentiment. Do you know how God sees you and who you are in Christ?

3

DO YOU KNOW HOW GOD SEES YOU? DO YOU KNOW WHO YOU ARE IN CHRIST?

Now that we have become a Christian, what should we be thinking about ourselves? Do you continue to think of yourself according to a particular pattern of behavior, or are you learning how to think about yourself in light of God's new perspective concerning you?

Let's begin by answering the following question.

How did God think about us before we were saved?

Let's find out by going to the book of Ephesians.

Ephesians 2:2-3

> *Wherein in time past ye walked according to the course of this world, according to the prince of the power of the air, the spirit that now worketh in the children of disobedience: Among whom also we all had our conversation in times past in the lusts of our flesh, fulfilling the desires of the*

flesh and of the mind; and were by nature the children of wrath, even as others.

Since we were born, our condition was that of spiritual death, being separated from God, and as such, we regulated our life within the sphere of trespasses and sins[12] in this moral and immoral atmosphere in accordance with the ruler of the demons. It's the spirit (the evil tendency; the disposition) of such that influences the children of disobedience (those who are disobedient in their nature; the unregenerate). The Apostle Paul further stated to the saints at Ephesus that at one time, their way of life was like the unrighteous, the unregenerate, who were habitually [performing acts] that satisfy the passions of the evil nature and of the evil thoughts, thus a fulfilling of those desires.[13]

So, before we were saved, we were known by God as being the children of disobedience, the children of wrath, i.e., as those who were unregenerate.

How else were we characterized before we were saved?

Please go to the book of 1 Corinthians.

1 Corinthians 6:9

Know ye not that the unrighteous shall not inherit the kingdom of God? Be not deceived: neither fornicators, nor idolaters, nor adulterers, nor effeminate, nor abusers of themselves with mankind,

We're told that the unrighteous (the unsaved; those not related to Christ; those who did INJUSTICE to others and attempted to do it under the sanction of the courts[14]) won't enter into the Kingdom of God (a heavenly newness of life; God's kingdom within; formed anew by the Spirit). And neither will the rest of those mentioned, not because of their sin, but because they were not saved. There were some sexual tendencies or inclinations mentioned here that some, who didn't know God, could be engaged in, such as those who are fornicators (those who have sex outside of marriage), adulterers (sex with someone who is not your husband or wife), effeminate (a male prostitute; the passive ... partners in a homosexual relationship[15]), and abusers of themselves with mankind (active partners in a homosexual relationship[16]). What I wanted you to notice was that the ones who were not saved were addressed as being unrighteous and/or by the sexual tendency or inclination in which they were engaged.

So, now that we're Christians, how does God see us or talk about us differently?

Stay in 1 Corinthians.

1 Corinthians 6:11

> *And such were some of you: but ye are washed, but ye are sanctified, but ye are justified in the name of the Lord Jesus, and by the Spirit of our God.*

Before we become aware of the words God uses when He talks about us, we need to know the basis for His divine name-calling of us; the basis of which is founded on our new condition that took place at salvation. The Apostle Paul told the converts at the church of Corinth that some of them used to practice some of the overt sins mentioned. However, at salvation, three things happened to them as to their spiritual condition.

- First, they were washed.

They were baptized by the Spirit into the Christian faith, being identified with Christ in His death and burial, thus being separated from sin's power. Likewise, they were identified with Him in His resurrection and became a new creation in order to be able to walk in newness of life by the same power that raised Him from the dead.

- Second, they were sanctified.

They were separated from common, earthly, or sinful uses, to be wholly employed in the service of the true God.[17]

- Third, they were justified.

They were accepted as righteous, having entered into a new relationship with God.

What we can deduce is that before salvation, such were all of us in the sense of committing sinful actions. However, all things have now become new. *Whom we used to be in the sight of God is no longer.* This doesn't mean that we're not susceptible to committing sins, but we have a new standing with God, a new nature, the indwelling Spirit, and the Word of God to help us learn how to be an overcomer in these or any areas of weakness.

Now that our condition in the sight of God has changed, what words does He use when He talks about us?

Please go to 2 Corinthians.

2 Corinthians 5:17

> *Therefore if any man be in Christ, he is a new creature: old things are passed away; behold, all things are become new.*

We're described as being a new creature, a new [creation,] a new being, a new person on the inside.[18] And as such, those things that characterized the pre-Christian life[19] have disappeared, and our whole sphere of being has become new, whom God the Father owns as his workmanship, and which He can look on and pronounce very good.[20]

How else are we looked upon by God? The next stop will be the book of Galatians.

Galatians 4:7

> *Wherefore thou art no more a servant, but a son; and if a son, then an heir of God through Christ.*

This tells us that we're no longer servants to sin or owe servitude to obey the tenets of the Mosaic Law. At salvation, we have become sons, adopted sons, adult sons positionally – as God declares it; a member of His family. And because we are His sons, we're heirs who possess God Himself, who can partake of His nature, and who possess every spiritual blessing to which we're entitled. Beautiful isn't it. Do you think of yourself in this manner?

Go forward to the book of Ephesians.

Ephesians 2:19

> *Now therefore ye are no more strangers and foreigners, but fellowcitizens with the saints, and of the household of God;*

Who are we, as this verse so beautifully puts it? We're no longer those who had no kind of rights like the unconverted Gentiles when they left their country and entered the territory of the Jews, but when our conversion took place, we're not only as those who belong to the same community with the same heavenly citizenship of the Christianized Jews, but we're also of the household of God, i.e., of the same family having all equal rights, privileges, and advantages; as all, through one Spirit.[21]

Is this helping you with respect to how you should see yourself and thus expect the same perception by your fellow believers?

The final question is, when we operate in sin, does the sin characterize us, i.e., as being a fornicating Christian, an adulterous Christian, a lying Christian, a gay Christian, etc.?

Let's begin by going to the book of 1 Corinthians.

1 Corinthians 3:1

And I, brethren, could not speak unto you as unto spiritual,
but as unto carnal, even as unto babes in Christ.

The Apostle Paul is informing us that a Christian can be characterized by the nature in which they are operating, which would essentially signify the level of their spiritual growth or walk with God. He said to the Christians at Corinth that he could not speak unto them as unto spiritual, i.e., spiritually mature, as those who allow the Spirit to teach him [them] and direct him [them] by feeding on the Word.[22] Unfortunately, he had to speak to them as those who were carnal, i.e., characterized as spiritually immature as evidenced by being wholly under the influence of his [their] sensual …nature.[23] The reason given for them being in this state was that they had a want of capacity to digest and assimilate good strong food of truth.[24] And as such, they were considered to be like children as relates to their understanding of Christian teachings,[25] i.e., they lived on "Bible stories" and not Bible doctrines.[26]

What else do the Scriptures have to say about us when we're operating in sin?

Please go to the book of 1 Corinthians.

. . .

1 Corinthians 5:11

> *But now I have written unto you not to keep company, if any man that is called a brother be a fornicator, or covetous, or an idolater, or a railer, or a drunkard, or an extortioner; with such an one no not to eat.*

> *Romans 6:3-4 Know ye not, that so many of us as were baptized into Jesus Christ were baptized into his death? Therefore we are buried with him by baptism into death: that like as Christ was raised up from the dead by the glory of the Father, even so we also should walk in newness of life.*

It's possible for a Christian to habitually engage in certain sins such as those committed by a fornicator (a male prostitute; a man who indulges in unlawful sexual intercourse[27]), or covetous (greedy), or an idolater (one who eats things offered to idols), or railer (slanderer; someone who speaks insultingly or abusively of others[28]), or a drunkard (addicted to alcoholic consumption), or an extortioner (one who carries off the possessions of another by force[29]).

If a Christian commits any of these sins, could they be called by others as being a fornicator, covetous, etc.?

The answer is yes. However, who they are in Christ and the sin they are committing is to remain separable. I hope that you understand what was just said. A verse that supports this perspective is found in the book of 1 John.

1 John 3:9

> *Whosoever is born of God doth not commit sin; for his seed*

> *remaineth in him: and he cannot sin, because he is born of God.*

This is a very interesting verse pertaining to the committing of sin by a Christian. It says that whosoever is born of God (is permanently spiritually alive) does not continually choose to commit sin because God's seed (divine life) abides in him/her. And furthermore, the child of God cannot sin because sin can never spring from whom a Christian truly is. So, this is telling us that a Christian can't sin, whether habitually or not, in terms of who they have become at salvation because this spiritual reality separates the sin from the believer's position in Christ.

After reading this, a Christian might think they can never sin. This is indeed not the case. Another way of saying this is, when a Christian is walking in the Spirit, he/she cannot sin. Sin can never spring from the divine life or nature received when we're operating in it. Remember, at salvation, we receive a new nature, but this doesn't remove the old sin nature. *As to our identity, there's a clear difference between saying that a Christian is committing fornication than saying that he/she is a fornicating Christian.* I hope that this helps in better understanding this distinction.

There's another verse that tells us that if a Christian commits criminal behavior, then he/she could be charged as and being so.[30]

The final verse to be looked at is found in the book of 1 Peter.

1 Peter 4:15

> *But let none of you suffer as a murderer, or as a thief, or as an evildoer, or as a busybody in other men's matters.*

The Apostle Peter is imploring fellow believers that hopefully none of them would be charged and as being so[31] a murderer (homicide), a thief (confiscation of property was not to be compensated for by theft[32]), an evildoer (some other kind of criminal action toward others), or as a busybody in other men's matters (breach of confidence, perpetrated for profit or to gain some unfair or dishonest advantage;[33] one who pries into the affairs of another; one who attempts to control or direct them as if they were his own;[34] "bishop" ... of other men's matters - of things that [don't] concern him[35]).

If we commit certain criminal offenses, we'll be charged and determined as being someone who commits such. If we steal, we'll be referred to as being a thief, but there's no such thing as a thieving Christian. In Christ, all things are new. Regrettably, we still have a sin nature, and at times we'll operate in it. This doesn't change who we're in Christ, and neither does it describe who we're in Christ. I hope you get the point. So, start changing the way you think about yourself.

God doesn't consider you or me as being a fornicating Christian, an adulterous Christian, a lying Christian, a gay Christian even when we're engaged in such behavior. So, stop thinking about yourself in this way. Learn how God thinks about you and reflect upon it. Learn about who you are in Christ and begin to appropriate this divine perspective for yourself. Learn how to replace a false perception of yourself according to the passions and inclinations of the sin nature and replace it with the true perception of yourself according to God's Word.

This brings us to the place of addressing the final comment made by a believer in the evangelical church, which was, "... people don't recognize that any relationship that I have with a man is part of God's plan and that it would be full of love, equal to any other."[36]

There are two things to consider in attempting to address this comment. What is God's plan for my life, and what kind of sexual relationships does the Word of God condone? We'll begin by attempting to answer the first question, and that is, what is God's plan for my life?

4

WHAT IS GOD'S WILL OR PLAN FOR MY LIFE?

What is God's will or plan for our life? There are two ways we could answer this. The first is the general plan meaning that it involves certain spiritual attainments to which God would have each of us aspire. The second is the particular plan, which involves the Holy Spirit working individually in each of our lives to provide us with guidance in many areas. That would include finances, friendships, marriage partners, where we should reside geographically, the conviction of sin, illumination of Scripture, exercising our spiritual gifts, etc. Which one should we focus on initially? I believe the general one. Why? Because as you will see, if we're able to participate in God's general plan, this will provide for us the proper foundation for His individual plan for our life.

GOD'S GENERAL PLAN

What are those scriptural declarations which are considered as a part of God's general plan for our life?

We'll begin in the book of Romans.

. . .

Romans 8:29-30

> *For whom he did foreknow, he also did predestinate to be conformed to the image of his Son, that he might be the firstborn among many brethren. Moreover whom he did predestinate, them he also called: and whom he called, them he also justified: and whom he justified, them he also glorified.*

God the Father knew beforehand (*foreknowledge*), who would respond to His invitation of salvation by repenting and believing in His Son as to who He is and what He has accomplished. Therefore, He chose (*elected*) whosoever beforehand (before they were ever born). In time, God instituted His plan called *predestination*. This involves many events, as well as the decisions that mankind would make, especially concerning salvation. The goal of predestination is for people to become saved and subsequently fulfill God's plan for their life.

If we were living during the time when Israel first became a nation, the Age of Israel, we would be talking about God executing a plan through the institution of the Mosaic Law that would allow the Jews to believe in Him as He was revealed. But because we're living in the time of the church, we'll be talking about a plan that has to do with people responding to the gospel message. In this dispensation, once a person is saved, one of God's desires for him/her is to be conformed to the image of His Son.

What does it mean for a Christian to be conformed to the image of God's Son?

The word *conformed* refers to the process of sanctification, whereby the saint is transformed in his [her] inner heart life to resemble.[37] To resemble what or whom? That they should resemble the image of God's Son. The word *image* refers to character. Where is this idea of character derived from in Scripture? It's found in the book of Galatians.

. . .

Galatians 5:22-23

> *But the fruit of the Spirit is love, joy, peace, longsuffering, gentleness, goodness, faith, Meekness, temperance: against such there is no law.*

The word *fruit* means the Spirit's influences, spiritual qualities, or graces which relate to Christian character, or the unity of the character of the Lord.

So, there you have it. One of the goals of God's general plan for us is that we would be conformed (i.e., a transformation would take place in our inner heart life) whereby we resemble the image (the likeness; the character) of the Lord. This character refers to the fruit, the graces, or the spiritual qualities of the Holy Spirit.

What else is considered a part of God's general plan for our life?

Please go to the book of 1 Thessalonians.

1 Thessalonians 4:1-4

> *1 Furthermore then we beseech you, brethren, and exhort you by the Lord Jesus, that as ye have received of us how ye ought to walk and to please God, so ye would abound more and more. 2 For ye know what commandments we gave you by the Lord Jesus.*

Paul declared to the saints of the church at Thessalonica that as they received (learned) from him, Silvanus, and Timotheus as to how they ought to walk (behave toward one another) so as to please God, the hope for this quality of life is that it would abound (increase) more and more. He then reminded them to recall the commandments (the instructions) regarding personal purity (as to how they should live). And then he proceeded to tell them the will of God for their lives.

3 For this is the will of God, even your sanctification, that ye should abstain from fornication:

The will or general plan of God for their lives is their sanctification (that they should be holy).

How is sanctification accomplished?

4 That every one of you should know how to possess his vessel in sanctification and honour;

This is accomplished when each of them is able to learn and know how[38] *to possess* (be controlled through God's power; gain mastery; exercise self-control) over *his vessel* (his body; his sexual desires) *in sanctification* (behavior that is set apart to the Lord in its motivation) *and honour* (recognized by others as intrinsically worthy of respect[39]).

While we're not told how to possess (gain mastery over) our body (sexual desires), we're told that this is God's will or plan for the life of every Christian.

There's one more very important spiritual reality that is God's general will or plan for our lives.

This is found in the book of Ephesians.

Ephesians 5:18

And be not drunk with wine, wherein is excess; but be filled with the Spirit

We're commanded to be filled with the Spirit. The word *filled* refers to the believer being under the Spirit's control. It also suggests the idea that this condition occurs because the believer has yielded him/herself to Him. And when we're yielded to Him, He is said to control us in our mind, emotions, and will.[40] As we learn how to consistently be under His rule, we'll increasingly manifest His fruit.

This doesn't tell us how we get to be yielded to Him, but what it does convey to us is when we are, we'll be evidencing to others His spiritual qualities of character.

Some would say there's so much more to what God's general will or plan is for our lives. They will stress obedience to God's Word as it pertains to street witnessing, prayer, laying down our lives for one another, visiting the orphan and widows, providing financially, etc. While I would agree that we should be responsive to these opportunities to express Christ-likeness to others, I would also contend that without learning how to be conformed to the image of God's Son, how to have mastery over our sexual desires, and how to be filled with the Spirit all the actions that we attempt to perform will be done in self-power according to the inclinations of the flesh. Instead of revealing Christ-likeness to others, we'll only reveal the person we used to be before we were saved. So, what we're really talking about here is our testimony; as to whether it's reflective of the old sin nature or the new spiritual nature.

Does our testimony come from obedience to God's Word and translate to doing this or doing that? Or should our testimony start from within? Being transformed from within will reveal Christ-likeness in everything we do. A lack of inward transformation will expose what appears to be godly actions before those in leadership and our fellow believers by being void of godly character that exemplifies the fruit of the Spirit.

Now that we know what the general will or plan of God is for our life let's take a look at an attempt to address the second part of the final comment that someone who attended the church ministry expressed in the article, "Sex Abuse & Gay Conversion Therapy: The Dark Past of Justin Bieber's Megachurch Hillsong."[41] The second part of the final comment is, there are people who don't recognize that any relationship that I have with a man ... would be full of love, equal to any other.[42] In response to this, what needs to be understood are the specifics of God's plan. This believer was saying that he considered his relationship with a man as being part of God's plan. When we become saved, there are a lot of things that [we're] not sure about as to whether we should continue in them or not. Am I allowed to continue to drink alcohol? Am I allowed to get a divorce? What about having a relationship outside of marriage?

Where do we find the answers to these questions? We find them in five avenues: (1) attending a church that teaches on these topics (2) reading Christian books (3) watching a pertinent video on such (4) the Bible and (5) our own study of the Scriptures.

The question [we're] really attempting to answer based on the second part of this believer's comment is, what is God's perspective concerning sexual relationships now that we have become a Christian?

When Jesus said, to love one another, as I have loved you in John 15:12, does this mean that the love we should be operating in condones fornication, adultery, homosexuality, pedophilia, etc.?

Like any other question that you or I have, the answer should be found in the Scriptures. The Epistles, which are letters written to the fledgling churches and individual believers in the earliest days of Christianity, contains answers to what constitutes sinful behavior, how we're to act toward fellow believers and unbelievers concerning it, and how we can grow spiritually.

Are you ready to take a look at what the Word of God says and find out what it means to love one another with God's love?

5

WHAT DOES IT MEAN TO LOVE ONE ANOTHER WITH GOD'S LOVE?

GOD'S SPECIFIC PLAN

Now that we know what God's general plan is for the believer, we need to learn what His specific plan is all about. In this particular instance, we're looking to address the opinion of a male who was involved in a Christian megachurch that expressed his belief about having a relationship with another man that he contends would be full of love like any other relationship between two adults.

It's understandable when some Christians are not sure as to whether operating in God's love condones fornication, adultery, homosexuality, lesbianism, etc. Like any other biblical topic, we need to be taught by someone in leadership as to what Scripture has to say about this. I'm not writing on this study entitled TESTIMONY to give you my opinions, but what Scripture has to say on this topic.

What I've found out in attempting to determine what are the characteristics and expressions of God's love is that there are other words that are used in

Scripture to denote affection. So, what we'll attempt to do is look at each of these and try to determine which ones reflect godly qualities and actions and which ones don't.

The first one we'll look at pertains to God's love.

AGAPE LOVE

Agape is the noun form, and *agapao* is the verb form.

What kind of love is this?

When we consider how Christians operate in this love, what are the thoughts and actions that they should be thinking and expressing toward others?

Please go to the book of Galatians.

Galatians 5:22-23

> *But the fruit of the Spirit is love, joy, peace, longsuffering, gentleness, goodness, faith, Meekness, temperance: against such there is no law.*

This is God's love that is a fruit of the Spirit. The word *fruit*, which we talked about earlier in this study, can also mean elements of character. There are nine elements of character that God wants to produce in us, become operational in us, and be expressive to others. The first element of character is called love. The Greek rendering of this word in the noun form is transliterated (to change letters from one language to another) into English and written as *agape*.

Because most of our English New Testament is derived from Koine Greek (the common language of the Greeks during the time of Christ) and in certain minimal instances Aramaic, all we need to do is find this particular word *love* in Scripture by using a concordance, which will indicate to us every place it appears. We'll also be able to find out whether this word was used to signify God's *agape* love or another expression for love. And along with this, wherever this word *love* appears, we'll be made aware as to whether it was used as a noun or verb.

So, this particular word for *love* means divine love, which is a love produced in the heart of the yielded believer by the Holy Spirit; its chief ingredient, self-sacrifice for the benefit of the one loved.[43]

Are you ready to find out more about what this word *love* means, whether in the form of a noun or a verb?

Please go to the book of 1 Corinthians.

Suggested Reading: 1 Corinthians 13:1-8

The word used as synonymous with the word *love* in these verses is *charity*, and it's used primarily as a noun. There's much to say about God's love when a Christian is operating in it toward others and whether the recipients of such are believers or unbelievers.

1 Corinthians 13:4 Charity suffereth long...

Charity (God's *agape* love) is patient in bearing the offenses and injuries of others. It has a long mind.[44] Stay with me in looking at another part of the same verse.

1 Corinthians 13:4 ...charity envieth not...

God's love is not [grieved] because another possesses a greater portion of earthly, intellectual, or spiritual blessings.[45] Take a look at the next verse, which follows this one.

1 Corinthians 13:5 ...seeketh not her own...

Charity does not seek one's own happiness to the injury of another.

To find out another perspective about God's love, please go to the book of Romans.

Romans 13:8

Owe no man any thing, but to love one another: for he that loveth another hath fulfilled the law.

This is an interesting verse, which talks about the fact that if we owe someone a debt, we must make sure we pay it back. Why? Because this is an expression of God's love in interpersonal relationships. God's love is responsible for its actions.

Go forward in your Bible to the book of 1 John.

1 John 3:16

Hereby perceive we the love of God, because he laid down his life for us: and we ought to lay down our lives for the brethren.

As we perceive (gain spiritual knowledge by experience) the love of God expressed in the laying down of His life for us, because of our response to such, we'll have become the recipients of salvation.[46] And likewise, we should lay down our life (by giving our time, care, prayers, substance[47]) for the brethren.

What else can we learn about God's love?

1 John is where we should go next.

Suggested Reading: 1 John 4:7-19

7 Beloved, let us love one another: for love is of God; and every one that loveth is born of God, and knoweth God.

The Apostle John instructed believers to habitually love one another (be ready to promote each other's welfare, both spiritual and temporal[48]).

The next verse talks about God's love operating in marriage.

Ephesians 5:25

> *Husbands, love your wives, even as Christ also loved the church, and gave himself for it;*

Husbands are instructed by the Apostle Paul to love their wives (to give himself in self-sacrifice for the well-being of the one who is loved;[49] to promote the salvation of their wives, and their constant edification in righteousness;[50] to seek the highest good for another person[51]), even as Christ loved the church and gave of Himself to redeem it.

Let's proceed onward to the book of Galatians.

Galatians 5:13

> *For, brethren, ye have been called unto liberty; only use not liberty for an occasion to the flesh, but by love serve one another.*

Brethren, you *have been called unto liberty* (through the Spirit free from the power of sin in his daily life; and free from the Law with its demands and threats[52]). *Only use not this liberty for an occasion to the flesh* (to indulge the sinful nature or as a furtherance to corrupt passions[53]), but by the *love* of the Spirit (divine love; [such love] means death to self, and that means defeat for [sin] since the essence of sin is self-will and self-gratification[54]) *serve one another* (to do that which is for the advantage of someone else[55]).

Now that we know some of the thought patterns and subsequent expressions of divine love, the next question we can seek an answer for will help us determine what is contrary to it.

What are the thought patterns and subsequent expressions that are contrary to divine love, which a Christian should no longer be entertaining in their mind and thus committing in their actions?

Let's begin by going to the book of 1 John.

1 John 2:15-16

> *15 Love not the world, neither the things that are in the world. If any man love the world, the love of the Father is not in him.*

God's love commands us as to what we should not love. We're not to love *the world* (the ordered system of which Satan is the head, his fallen angels and demons are his emissaries, and the unsaved of the human race are his subjects, together with those purposes, pursuits, pleasures, practices, and places where God is not wanted.[56]

> *16 For all that is in the world, the lust of the flesh, and the lust of the eyes, and the pride of life, is not of the Father, but is of the world.*

We're also commanded to not love what *is in the world,* which consists of *the lust* (sensual and impure desires) *of the flesh* (of the depraved nature), and *the lust* (the mental pleasure) *of the eyes, and the pride of life* (includes the desire to gain credit which does not belong to us, and outshine our [neighbors];[57] an insolent and vain assurance in one's own resources, or in the stability of earthly things[58]).

What stood out to me is that we're commanded not to love the sensual and impure desires of the depraved nature. And we can speculate that whatever these desires are that may occupy us will express themselves in sensual and impure actions. What actions are considered sensual and impure in Scripture? Keep on reading, and hopefully, we'll find out.

I don't know about you, but I found learning about God's *agape* love enlightening. Here is a summary of it.

God's *agape* love:

1. Self-sacrifices for the benefit of someone else.
2. Operating in a husband seeks the spiritual well-being of his wife.
3. Is patient in bearing the offenses and injuries of others.
4. Is not grieved because another possesses a greater portion of earthly, intellectual, or spiritual blessings.[59]
5. Does not seek one's own happiness to the injury of another.
6. Lays down its life (by giving our time, care, prayers, substance[60]) for the brethren.
7. Does not operate in the sin nature and continue in corrupt passions.
8. Does not love the sensual and impure desires of the depraved nature.
9. Is not kindled by the merit or worth of its object, but it originates in its own God-given nature.[61]
10. Does not find assurance in one's own resources or in earthly things.

Did you know that there's another word for love that Scripture mentions? Any idea what this love is all about? Let's find out.

PHILIA LOVE

Philia, a noun, is the transliteration of the Greek word. The verb form is *phileo.*

What is Philadelphia love all about?

How is it different from *agape* love?

Please go to the book of Titus.

Titus 2:4

> *That they may teach the young women to be sober, to love their husbands, to love their children,*

Titus was instructing the aged Christian women (those advanced in years) that they *teach the young* Christian *women,* who are married, *to be sober* (to have their desires and passions well-regulated or under proper control[62]), *to philia love their husbands* (not be fond of other men than their own), and *to philia love their children* (maternal affection; used to describe feelings or actions which are typical of those of a kind mother [toward] her child[63]). This love is described as being that of a *philia* type of love, a love for one's family.

Why wasn't this love mentioned as being *agape*?

I can only assume, based on what we know about *agape* love is that it's a love that is self-sacrificing, i.e., it loves irrespective of the person loved or their response to it, whereas *philia* love appears to be a love based on something about the person who is loved which causes us to love them. Let's see if what I just said is true about *philia* love by looking at more verses where this type of love is being illustrated.

The book of 1 Peter is where we should go next.

1 Peter 1:22

> *Seeing ye have purified your souls in obeying the truth through the Spirit unto unfeigned love of the brethren, see that ye love one another with a pure heart fervently:*

Apparently, there were some Christians who had issues with *philia* loving their fellow believers. Unfortunately, they were operating in feigned (hypocritical) love. This love was described as being like a mask of feigned love placed over their usual countenances when associating with certain others of their brethren.[64] Their only way out of living in this counterfeit love was by continual obedience to God's Word while operating under the influences of the Holy Spirit.

By choosing to appropriate and think with God's Word, this caused them to operate in the fruit of the Spirit, and as such, they evidenced God's love toward their brethren, which was characterized as being a *philia* unfeigned love (an unhypocritical love). This love is characterized as liking someone else because that person is like himself [herself] in the sense that this person reflects in his (her) own personality the same characteristics, the same likes and dislikes that he [she] himself [herself] has[65]). Based on the context, these characteristics would be those exemplified by the Word of God.

Then, the Apostle Peter said to them to see to it that they *agape love one another with a pure* [not for the love of ourselves; to not use for our advantage; free from hypocrisy (a pretense of having a virtuous character[66])] *heart* (mind) *fervently* (in an all-out manner).

This is interesting in that both *philia* and *agape* love are mentioned in the same verse. This seems to be saying that we should always be operating in divine love toward our fellow believers. And when we love them, because of something about them, this love can be described as a *philia* type love of the brethren.

Where should we go next? How about the book of 1 Thessalonians?

1 Thessalonians 4:9

> *But as touching brotherly love ye need not that I write unto you: for ye yourselves are taught of God to love one another.*

This verse talks about both *agapao* divine and *philia* brotherly love.

The reason why I included it is that in this context, it's referred to as a love that is shown in relieving distressed brethren.[67]

So, to recap, *philia* love is a deep friendship kind of love, where we love the brethren or a family member because that person is like ourselves as to our personality or they have the same likes or dislikes that we do. We could also say that this love is called out of one's heart by qualities in another.[68]

Is there any other Greek word for love that we need to look at?

Believe it or not, there's another one. Are you ready to take a look at this?

STERGE LOVE

Sterge is the noun form, and *stergo* is the verb form.

How can this type of love be explained?

Please go to the book of Romans.

Romans 12:9-10

> *9 Let love be without dissimulation. Abhor that which is evil; cleave to that which is good.*

The Apostle Paul was instructing the believers at Rome that their *agape love be without dissimulation* (without hypocrisy; a love that puts self aside in an effort to help and bless others. Yes, a love that goes to the point of suffering if that is necessary in order to bless others[69]). They were also instructed to *Abhor* (turn away from) *that which is evil* (whatever is unkind or injurious to a brother[70]) and to *cleave* (hold fast) *to that which is good* (sharing the burdens and the blessing of others so that we all grow together and glorify the Lord[71]).

> 10 *Be kindly affectioned one to another with brotherly love; in honour preferring one another;*

Along with this, they were admonished to show tender affection *to one another with philia storge brotherly love* (the warmth of family affection[72]). One evidence of such is in showing *honour* (respect shown [to] another which is measured by one's evaluation of another[73]) by *preferring one another* (every act of friendly kindness[74]).

In this context, we're to *agape* love the brethren with genuine love and *philia storge* family affection. Believe it or not, *storge* love, the love for one's family, is found nowhere else in the Epistles. You might ask, then how do you know that it means family love? We can determine this by finding out what the antitheses of this word means. The antithesis Greek word *astorgos* means to be heartless, without affection to kindred, and lacking natural love among family members. The transliteration of this Greek word is found in only two places in Scripture, where the words *without natural affection* refer to the lack of love in the family.

> *Romans 1:31 Without understanding, covenant breakers, without natural affection, implacable, unmerciful:*

> *2 Timothy 3:3 Without natural affection, trucebreakers, false accusers, incontinent, fierce, despisers of those that are good,*

We can conclude, therefore, that *storge* love is natural family affection for husband, wife, child, and fellow believers.

I know you are not going to believe this, but there's one more word in Greek that refers to love. Really? What kind of love?

EROS LOVE

Eros is the noun form, and *eros* is the verb form.

. . .

This kind of love is passionate love. It's comprised of pleasure. The basic idea of this love is self-satisfaction.[75] This love looks for whatever it is in another person that makes them happy. If for whatever reason that which makes one happy is gone or has somehow changed into that which is undesirable, then this love no longer expresses itself toward the other person and subsequently seeks someone else to make them happy.

The transliteration of the original Greek word, which in its English form is *eros,* is not found in the New Testament. However, I do think that the way to characterize this kind of love is that of it being a sensual love, which in the expression of its action could be considered moral or immoral based on societal norms. *Are societal norms God's norms? If society approves of a certain sexual behavior, does this mean that God's people should approve of it?*

Based on this study on the four different types of love according to the Koine Greek language, we have learned that each of these has its own characteristics. We know that God would desire for us to operate in His *agape* love toward believers and unbelievers, *philia* friendship brotherly love, and in *storge* love toward family. But what about *eros* love? Does He desire for us to operate in this type of love, which is a sensual type love that could seek its pleasure in such sexual avenues as marriage, polygamy, fornication, prostitution, adultery, homosexuality, lesbianism, incest, and pedophilia?

You should know the drill by now. The only way to answer this question or any other pertaining to whatever the topic is to find out what Scripture says about these sexual practices. But before we do, let's take a look at societal norms concerning sexual behavior. I think this would be an interesting avenue that will allow us to gain perspective on one very important principle. What is that principle, you ask? Please go to the next chapter and find out.

6

SHOULD A CHRISTIAN FOLLOW SOCIETAL NORMS CONCERNING SEXUAL BEHAVIOR?

There are probably many examples of societal norms pertaining to sexual behavior that we could present. Instead of overkill on this subject, let's just mention a couple of them.

Let's begin by taking a look at some articles that I found online pertaining to sexuality. This one has to do with the Romans during the time of Christ.

---

3 AWFUL FEATURES OF ROMAN SEXUAL MORALITY

Roman Sexuality Was [about] Dominance

Sexuality was tied to ideas of masculinity, male domination, and the adoption of the Greek pursuit of beauty.

Romans did not think in terms of sexual orientation. Rather, sexuality was tied to ideas of masculinity, male domination, and the adoption of the Greek pursuit of beauty. "In the Roman mind, the strong took what they wanted to take. It was socially acceptable for a strong Roman male to have intercourse with men or women alike, provided he was the aggressor. It was looked down upon to play the female 'receptive' role in homosexual liaisons."

A real man dominated in the bedroom as he did on the battlefield. He would have sex with his slaves whether they were male or female; he would visit prostitutes; he would have homosexual encounters even while married; he would engage in pederasty (see below); even rape was generally acceptable as long as he only raped people of a lower status. "He was strong, muscular, and hard in both body and spirit. Society looked down on him only when he appeared weak or soft." So, Romans did not think of people as being oriented toward homosexuality or heterosexuality. Instead, they understood that a respectable man would express his dominance by having sex—consensual or forced—with men, women, and even children.

Roman Sexuality Accepted

The pursuit of beauty and the obsession with the masculine ideal led to the widespread practice of pederasty—a sexual relationship between an adult man and an adolescent boy. This had been a common feature of the Greek world and was [adopted] by the Romans, who saw it as a natural expression of male privilege and domination. A Roman man would direct his sexual attention toward a slave boy or, at times, even a freeborn [child] and would continue to do so until the boy reached puberty. These relationships were seen as an acceptable and even idealized form of love, the kind of love that expressed itself in [poems, stories, and songs].

In the Roman [world,] a man's wife was often seen as beneath him and less than he was, but a sexual relationship with another male, boy or man, represented a higher form of intellectual love and engagement. It was a man joining with that which was his equal and who could, therefore, share experiences and ideas with him in a way he could not with a [woman.] Pederasty —pedophilia—was understood to be good and acceptable.

. . .

Roman Sexuality Had a Low View of

Women were not generally held in high regard in Roman culture. "Women were often seen as weak physically and mentally. They were inferior to men and existed to serve the men as little more than slaves at times." A woman's value was largely in her ability to bear [children,] and if she could not do so, she was quickly cast off. Because lifespans were short and infant mortality was high, women were often married off in their young teens to maximize the number of children they could bear.

When it came to sexual mores, women were held to a very different standard than men. Where men were free to carry on homosexual affairs and to commit adultery with slaves, prostitutes, and concubines, a woman caught in adultery could be charged with a crime. "The legal penalty for adultery allowed the husband to rape the male offender and then, if he desired, to kill his wife." Under [Augustus,] it even became illegal for a man to forgive his wife—he was forced to divorce her. "[It's] not enough to suggest that women were under-appreciated in Roman culture. There are many instances where they were treated as second-class human beings, slightly more honored than slaves."[76]

I think we would agree that in America [today,] most of society would not approve of pedophilia. What about homosexuality or lesbianism? Again, I think we would agree that in the [50s and 60s,] homosexuality or lesbianism was considered by society as being perverse, unnatural sexual acts between two people of the same sex. That was until the 1970s, which was called the 'Me Decade.' This was a time when many marginal groups continued their fight for equality. Over time, some forty plus years later, on June 26, 2015, in the case of *Obergefell v. Hodges*, the Supreme Court struck down all state bans on same-sex marriage.

With these thoughts in mind, there's confusion in many churches as to whether to sanction marriages between two people of the same sex or not. Here are two articles that pertain to such. The first has to do with a mainstream church in the USA. The second has to do with the Church in Wales.

WHY A VOTE ON GAY CLERGY AND SAME-SEX MARRIAGE COULD SPLIT THE UNITED METHODIST CHURCH

The church is considering a proposal to end its prohibitions on same-sex marriage and ordaining gays and lesbians, but a rival plan to keep those policies in place appears to have more support.

The United Methodist Church is meeting in St. Louis this week to vote on whether to strengthen or end its prohibitions on same-sex marriage and ordaining gays and lesbians — a decision that could splinter the church.

The denomination has been grappling for years with how to respond to social changes that have buffeted other mainline Protestant congregations, with individual United Methodist churches adopting contradictory — and sometimes competing — practices. At some churches, clergy members have come out as gay or lesbian from the pulpit, while other pastors have preached that homosexuality is a sin.

With [twelve] million adherents worldwide, including seven million in the United States, the church gathered [eight hundred sixty-four] members in St. Louis to vote on the way forward.

But the meeting has laid bare the denomination's fissures. "The church," said Gideon Salatan, a member from the [Philippines, "Is] grievously wounded."

Here's a look at the two leading proposals, known [as] the Traditional Plan and the One Church Plan. No matter which garners the most votes, there are fears that significant numbers of people will be dissatisfied with the [outcome,] and many will ultimately leave.

What is the Traditional Plan?

This proposal essentially maintains the church's practice of denying gays and lesbians equality and appears to have the most support. The church's policy, which dates from 1972, states that "[The] practice of homosexuality is incompatible with Christian teaching."

The plan prohibits gays and lesbians from becoming clergy and forbids same-sex marriage. It defines homosexuals as people in same-sex marriages or civil [unions] and those who "publicly state that they are practicing homosexuals."

Clergy who officiate at same-sex weddings would receive a [one-year] unpaid suspension. A second offense would result in removal from the clergy.

The policy would also require groups within the denomination to "certify adherence" to the rule. Those who refuse would be "urged" to leave the United Methodist Church, which would prohibit them from using the denomination's name or logo.

The primary supporters of the proposal are church members from African nations and the Philippines, as well as evangelical Europeans and Americans, who expressed a desire to retain the church's longstanding rules.

"I was born into a traditional church, so [I'm] learning [what God's will is]," Julia Stukalova, a church member from Russia, said Monday. "God loves everyone, but he wants everyone to live according to his word."

And what's the alternative?

The One Church Plan would allow individual churches or regions to decide for themselves whether to hire gay clergy or to perform same-sex weddings.

It would also eliminate the church policy that homosexuality is incompatible with Christianity. Churches that choose not to hire gay and lesbian pastors or to conduct same-sex weddings would not be punished. Bishops and clergy who choose not to officiate at ordinations or same-sex weddings would be protected from being sanctioned.

The majority of support for the proposal comes from self-identified progressives, many of whom are from the United States.

"I will be very sad not to be able to claim the cross and the flame because [I'm] being kicked out," said Cheryl Johnson Bell, a clergy member who said her family had been part of the church for five generations.

What's next for the church?

The church is scheduled to vote Tuesday about which plan to pursue.

If the Traditional Plan is successful, some places, particularly in California, would probably begin preparing to leave the United Methodist Church, according to church members.

If the One Church Plan prevails, congregations in Africa and Asia might start preparing to form an independent Methodist church.

Any exit, however, involves a fairly cumbersome process and would most likely not occur for several [months] or even years.

"[It's] true that some persons and some local churches have an interest in withdrawal and separation," said Kenneth Carter, president of the church's Council of Bishops. "Unfortunately, the losers will be the most vulnerable, who won't have the protection of a united church."[77]

EVANGELICALS PUSH FOR NEW BISHOP AFTER CHURCH IN WALES ALLOWS PASTORS TO BLESS GAY MARRIAGES

By Nicole Alcindor, CP Reporter

Evangelicals who hold to traditional Christian teaching on sexuality and marriage are pushing for a new bishop to be appointed in the Church in Wales following the results of an early September vote to allow pastors to bless same-sex marriages.

The Church in Wales, composed of six Anglican dioceses in the United Kingdom, does not allow clergy to conduct legally binding same-sex marriage ceremonies. However, in a Sept. 6 vote of 28 to 12 in favor with two abstentions, clergy were approved to host blessing ceremonies for same-sex unions in their churches.

On Monday, members of the Evangelical Fellowship within the Church in Wales expressed formal disagreement with the vote.

In a statement, EFCW addressed the Church in Wales Governing Body, asking for more "clarity and consistency" in the plan to protect and care for dissenting churches and leaders.

EFCW is calling for a new bishop, whom it said, can represent those who "hold to an understanding of the doctrine of marriage as only being between a man and a woman."

The fellowship further expressed that it finds that the Governing Body of the Church in Wales "no longer properly represents the convictions of the wider membership of the Church in Wales."

"[EFCW] deeply regrets the recent decision of the Governing Body to [authorize] a liturgy to bless same-sex civil marriages and partnerships [and] we [recognize] the difficulties faced by the bishops and others within the Church in Wales as they have wrestled to bring better pastoral provision for those who are LGBT," the statement reads.

The statement acknowledges that the [Church] has "not always engaged well" with the LGBT community by being "deeply insensitive" and "hurtful."

"This is something of which we repent unreservedly," the statement expressed. "The Good News of Jesus Christ is for all people, regardless of sexual orientation. However, the decision to introduce a rite allowing for the blessing of same-sex unions, while well-intentioned, is the wrong step for the Church to take."

The EFCW finds that the Church in Wales has "departed from" the apostolic faith as revealed in Scripture.

"The only biblical context for sexual activity is heterosexual marriage," the statement argued. "The new rite for the blessing of same-sex unions, which introduces liturgy permitting the blessing of same-sex civil marriages, has, de facto, changed the Church's doctrine on marriage."

EFCW also said they find that the approved vote has caused damage to the Church in Wales' relationship with "the majority of the provinces in the global Anglican Communion" — which has taken a stance "committed to an orthodox understanding of human sexuality."

Relationships with bishops and clerics who choose to perform such blessings are now "impaired," the statement stated.

"This decision has brought disunity to God's Church," EFCW added. "Such disunity is a grave and serious matter which grieves the heart of God. The decision [dishonors] those [who] persuaded that Scripture teaches that sexual activity is restricted to heterosexual marriage, have chosen to remain celibate, often at tremendous personal cost."

As a result of the vote, ECFW claims there are a "significant number of Welsh Anglicans" who are faced with the "tough decisions as to where their future spiritual home lies." There "have been and will be resignations from Clergy, Lay Readers, Worship Leaders, Church Wardens, Sunday School Teachers, and parishioners."

"A number have withdrawn their regular giving to their churches. Others are determined to remain in the Church in Wales structure. A significant number are seeking help and guidance on deciding their future in the Church in Wales," the statement adds.

"EFCW is committed to helping in this discernment process, including conversations with those offering alternative Anglican structures, and will continue to offer fellowship for all Evangelical Anglicans regardless of whether they stay in the Church in Wales or leave it."

While some clergy have been told that dissenting ministers won't have to surrender their church buildings for blessing services, the statement warns that other bishops "believe they can exercise their prerogative to insist that a same-sex blessing service take place in any building in their Diocese, regardless of the conscience of the local cleric."

"This needs clarity and consistency across the [province] with details on how dissenting PCCs, Lay Officers, congregations (as well as ministers) may be protected and cared for if they [don't] wish their church buildings to be available for such services," the statement asserts.

Even with the current "difficulties, [pain,] and grief," the fellowship assures that it will continue to place its "hope and trust in God."

"God has not abandoned Wales or His people," the statement concludes. "We pray for all those engaged in proclaiming Christ boldly and faithfully to this nation, for [it's] in Him that help and salvation are found."[78]

The principle in which I wanted us to gain perspective is the fact that society determines what is considered acceptable sexual moral behavior. And this consideration can change from generation to generation, from centuries to centuries. However, this question remains.

Should a Christian follow societal norms with respect to approving certain sexual behaviors, or is there another avenue that he/she should pursue?

7

WHAT SHOULD DETERMINE THE WAY A BELIEVER SHOULD THINK, SPEAK, AND ACT?

Should Christians follow societal norms or God's norms in the way they think, speak, and act?

This is the dilemma facing many Christians. We have become born-again. We have received the Holy Spirit into our lives, and subsequently, a new nature. Eventually, we find out that the way we have been thinking about ourselves, about others, and the circumstances of life are diametrically opposed to the way God would have us to think.

Irrespective of God's Word, we want to continue in our *eros* romantic, passionate love because we have a desire for it, it brings us pleasure, and maybe even because we consider God's view on this area of our life as being antiquated. And in whatever form or expression this love takes us, we believe that God will sanction it because it's between two people or maybe even more than two people, and how could God not sanction love between people, right?

It's not for me to determine what God should respect concerning what I think, speak, or act. Rather it's up to God to declare to me through His Word and by the leading and guiding of the Holy Spirit the way I should think, speak and act now that I've become a Christian, a new creature, His adopted son, or daughter.

As was asked in the title of this chapter, what should determine the way a believer should think, speak, and act?

Any idea as to what the answer is to this question? The following verse tells us so.

2 Timothy 3:16

> *All scripture is given by inspiration of God, and is profitable for doctrine, for reproof, for correction, for instruction in righteousness:*

This verse tells us that it's Scripture that provides for us the proper perspective as to how we as Christians should think, speak and act. The last part of the words of this verse *for instruction in righteousness* pertains to our study at hand. These words refer to instruction that produces proper behavior. So, there you have it.

In this regard, let's take a look at Scriptures from the New Testament and see what God's Word declares to us concerning those sexual behaviors that He condones and those that He doesn't.

We'll begin by going to the book of 1 Corinthians. These initial verses that we'll look at seem to clarify two expressions of sexual activity that God approves of and one expression that He doesn't.

1 Corinthians 7:1-2

> *1 Now concerning the things whereof ye wrote unto me: It is good for a man not to touch a woman.*

Some believe that this exhortation had to do with a letter the Apostle Paul received from those in the church at Corinth concerning issues relating to marriage. Paul talked about the fact that it was good for a man *not to touch a woman,* probably for three reasons. One, if he was called to be celibate in the plan of God for a period of time.

Second, if there was a desire for the sexual union, then they should not commit fornication (having sex outside of marriage) but get married (having sex within marriage). Third, in God's eyes, being celibate or getting married is a witness or testimony of God's approval of each condition.

> *2 Nevertheless, to avoid fornication, let every man have his own wife, and let every woman have her own husband.*

The Apostle Paul further emphasized the point that if you can't constrain yourself with the woman you are with, then avoid fornication (immorality), and let every single man enter into marriage with the woman he is with, and vice versa.

I think what is being said in these verses would allow us to conclude that God sanctions celibacy according to His plan and will and marriage between a man and a woman. And we could also deduce that fornication is not condoned. This is a start to finding out what sexual practices are approved by God for Christians to engage in and which ones are not.

The next book we'll take a look at is the book of Romans.

Suggested Reading: Romans 1:16-33

> *Romans 1:16 For I am not ashamed of the gospel of Christ: for it is the power of God unto salvation to every one that believeth; to the Jew first, and also to the Greek.*

The Apostle Paul in his writing to the saints at Rome began his letter by telling them that he longed to visit them and that he was *not ashamed of the gospel of Christ* (the Good News which relates to the Messiah, to His character, advent, preaching, death, resurrection, and ascension[79]) in that *it is the power* (the means) *of God unto salvation* to those (to save those) who believe.

And then he talked about those who have decided not to respond to the gospel, to whom God has made known to them that He exists, that He is real, being evidenced outwardly through the observation of the created universe and inwardly in their conscience. Yet, they still chose not to worship Him, and neither were they thankful. As they made the decision to disregard Him and live for themselves, they became wise in their own eyes. They considered themselves cultivated, skilled and learned, but sadly, such self-absorption can lead to doing shameful things.

> *Romans 1:24 Wherefore God also gave them up to uncleanness through the lusts of their own hearts, to dishonour their own bodies between themselves:*

So, *God also gave them up* (left them to their own self-determination[80]) *to uncleanness* (moral and spiritual depravity). Concerning this, He gave two examples of this type of sexual behavior.

> *Romans 1:26-27 For this cause God gave them up unto vile affections: for even their women did change the natural use into that which is against nature: And likewise also the men, leaving the natural use of the woman, burned in their lust one toward another; men with men working that which is unseemly, and receiving in themselves that recompence of their error which was meet.*

Some of the unbelieving women were given over to a diseased condition out of which lust sprang to *vile* (disgraceful) *affections* (passions). They changed the natural relations with men in marriage to unnatural relations with women to do that, which is against natural laws. Likewise, there were some men who left the natural relations with women to have relations with men, thus engaging in an all-out endeavor to satisfy their [totally depraved natures],[81] the result (penalty) of such would be that they would receive evil consequences and punishment from God.

> *Romans 1:28 And even as they did not like to retain God in their knowledge, God gave them over to a reprobate mind, to do those things which are not convenient;*

Furthermore, we're told that *God gave* (let them do what they pleased[82]) *them* (unbelievers) *over to a reprobate mind* (a mind that cannot form right judgments[83]) *to do those things which are not convenient* (which expressed itself in attitudes and actions that ought not to be done[84]).

A list of these attitudes and actions is presented in the following verses.

> *Romans 1:29-31 Being filled with all unrighteousness, fornication, wickedness, covetousness, maliciousness; full of envy, murder, debate, deceit, malignity; whisperers, Backbiters, haters of God, despiteful, proud, boasters, inventors of evil things, disobedient to parents, Without understanding, covenant breakers, without natural affection, implacable, unmerciful:*

There appears to be only one of these attitudes/actions that is associated with sexual conduct, and that is the word fornication (all sexual contact between the sexes which is beyond the bounds of lawful marriage[85]). After which, the Apostle Paul proclaimed what God's response was toward those unbelievers, who were habitually entertaining these attitudes and practicing these actions.

> *32 Who knowing the judgment of God, that they which commit such things are worthy of death, not only do the same, but have pleasure in them that do them.*

Who knowing (in their conscience) *the judgment of God* (the grand rule of right which God has revealed to every man[86]), that they who are habitually practicing these things will receive punishment from his hand.[87] We're not told what these consequences or judgments from God are, but what we have been made aware of is that these will be imposed on those who engage in such sexual actions, i.e., fornication, homosexuality, and lesbianism.

Does this proclamation on consequence and judgment hold true only for unbelievers? If someone becomes saved, does this mean that these attitudes and actions are sanctioned by God? Just keep on keeping on, and we'll find out.

The next section of Scriptures we'll look at will confirm two sexual actions that are condoned by God and two sexual actions that are not.

Please go to the book of 1 Timothy.

Suggested Reading: 1 Timothy 3:1-7

> *1 This is a true saying, If a man desire the office of a bishop, he desireth a good work.*

The Apostle Paul is talking about the possibility that if someone *desire* (seeks after) *the office of a bishop* (pastor), he desires *a good work* (an honorable office). As to this leadership office, there's much debate today as to what qualifies someone to be a pastor. In this particular book of the Bible, there's presented one divine skill associated with this office along with other qualifications. One of the qualifications pertaining to this office leadership gift concerns a sexual relationship that is condoned by God. Any idea which one this is?

> *2 A bishop then must be blameless, the husband of one wife, vigilant, sober, of good behaviour, given to hospitality, apt to teach;*

One of the qualifications for someone seeking the office of pastor is that he must be the husband of one wife. This is not to say that a single person cannot seek the office of the pastor. Does this mean that if he were divorced, he would be unable to seek this office? Validly divorced people who remarried were considered married to one spouse.[88] The keywords just mentioned are validly divorced.

There are two main issues at stake here. Some would say that the word *husband* clearly indicates that a pastor can only be a male. This is a study in and of itself. I've addressed this perception in a different study entitled, "Who Says Women Can't Lead? - *We have been told from the pulpit that only men have been called to the leadership positions of the church. - Uncovered truths and new translations have challenged this perspective.*"

The next issue to address is, what do the words *of one wife* mean? These words refer to the marital conditions that must be met for someone to be considered for this office. What are they, you ask? Those marital conditions that are allowed and those that are not allowed are listed below. Let's take a look at them.

Marital conditions that are allowed for a born-again Christian to seek the office of pastor.

- If a Christian is married to an unbeliever, and the unbeliever chooses to leave the marriage, then the believer is allowed to divorce and remarry. 1 Corinthians 7:15
- If a Christian is married to either a believer or unbeliever, who decides to engage in an extramarital affair, then the Christian is allowed to divorce and remarry. Matthew 19:9
- If the husband or wife dies, then the Christian is allowed to remarry. Romans 7:2
- If a Christian is married to a believer and the believer chooses to leave the marriage (separation, not divorce) while remaining unmarried without engaging in an extramarital affair, then the Christian is to remain unmarried or be reconciled to their spouse. 1 Corinthians 7:10-11

Marital conditions that are not allowed for a born-again Christian to seek the office of pastor.

- If the Christian seeks a divorce when their believing spouse chooses to leave the marriage (separation) while remaining unmarried without engaging in an extramarital affair. 1 Corinthians 7:10-11

What else could we assume from the qualification of being *the husband of one wife*? We could deduce that marriage is between one man and one woman. This would, therefore, not condone the practice of polygamy or marriage between people of the same gender.

With that said, the literal name of the sexual practice we'll take a look at next is not found in Scripture. However, there are examples of it in the Old and New Testaments. Any idea what this could be referring to? Let's begin by taking a look at the words used to describe it, along with those people who would be considered as engaged in such from the Old Testament.

Please go to the book of Leviticus.

Suggested Reading: Leviticus 18:1-16

Usually, when I do a study on most biblical topics that pertain to the Church Age, the age during which we Christians currently live, I don't use Scriptures from the Old Testament to support a New Testament perspective on doctrine. However, in this instance, because there are such limited examples of this sexual practice, I've decided to have us take a look at how the Jews under Moses' guidance viewed this. What is this sexual practice? Read on.

1 And the Lord spake unto Moses, saying,

. . .

The Lord (*Yahweh*) is instructing Moses to convey His thoughts on the sexual practice called incest to the children of Israel. Believe it or not, the transliteration of the Hebrew or Greek word for incest appears nowhere in the Old or New Testaments. When we think of incest today, probably many of us think of sexual relations between a brother and sister or even cousins. However, what we're about to find out, at least as far as the Old Testament goes, is that this involved more family members than first thought. Because I could find very little about this in the New Testament, why not at least take a look at what sexual relations were considered as incestual in the Old Testament.

> *6 None of you shall approach to any that is near of kin to him, to uncover their nakedness: I am the Lord.*

The words that are used in this context for incest are *near of kin*. Generally speaking, these words included the extended family as well as the immediate family.[89] Below are the many verses that pertain to the instances where sexual relations would be considered incest. Let's read them over, and then I will provide a clearer summary as to who was involved.

> *7 The nakedness of thy father, or the nakedness of thy mother, shalt thou not uncover: she is thy mother; thou shalt not uncover her nakedness.*
> *8 The nakedness of thy father's wife shalt thou not uncover: it is thy father's nakedness.*
> *9 The nakedness of thy sister, the daughter of thy father, or daughter of thy mother, whether she be born at home, or born abroad, even their nakedness thou shalt not uncover.*
> *10 The nakedness of thy son's daughter, or of thy daughter's daughter, even their nakedness thou shalt not uncover: for theirs is thine own nakedness.*
> *11 The nakedness of thy father's wife's daughter, begotten of*

thy father, she is thy sister, thou shalt not uncover her nakedness.

12 Thou shalt not uncover the nakedness of thy father's sister: she is thy father's near kinswoman.

13 Thou shalt not uncover the nakedness of thy mother's sister: for she is thy mother's near kinswoman.

14 Thou shalt not uncover the nakedness of thy father's brother, thou shalt not approach to his wife: she is thine aunt.

15 Thou shalt not uncover the nakedness of thy daughter in law: she is thy son's wife; thou shalt not uncover her nakedness.

16 Thou shalt not uncover the nakedness of thy brother's wife: it is thy brother's nakedness.

The wording of these verses could be confusing as to who is who. So, according to UBS [United Bible Society] Old Testament Handbook, incest could involve sexual relations of a son with his own mother; a son with his stepmother; a brother with his sister; a brother with his stepsister; a father with his son's or daughter's daughter (a grandchild); a son with his father's or mother's sister; a son with his father's brother's wife; a father with his son's wife; and a son with his brother's wife. Whew.

With this in mind, how do the New Testament Scriptures define incest?

Are the descriptions of what constitutes incest under Moses and the Jews the same for believers in the New Testament?

Are there any examples of incest in the New Testament?

There might be one that is found in the book of 1 Corinthians. Let's turn there.

1 Corinthians 5:1

It is reported commonly that there is fornication among you, and such fornication as is not so much as named among the Gentiles, that one should have his father's wife.

Here is an example of a man having been found out to have had sexual relations with his father's wife, who was actually his stepmother. At this time, I'm sure the Jewish faith would consider this as incest, and it probably would be looked upon as such in the same manner by the New Testament church unless Scripture declared otherwise. The consequence of this offense was that certain ones in the church met together and decided to impose censure on this believer, thus removing him from fellowship for a fixed period of time.

I assume that the reason he was not excommunicated was that he probably repented of this sin when he was brought before those of the assembly who were in charge of hearing such matters. And presumably, when the allotted time for him to be reinstated to fellowship was up that there would probably be those believers who could testify on his behalf as to whether or not he was continuing to engage in such sexual activity.

In the United States, laws regarding incest (i.e., sexual activity between family members or close relatives) vary considerably between jurisdictions. In all that two states (and the special case of Ohio, which "targets only parental figures"), incest between consenting adults is criminalized. In New Jersey and Rhode Island, incest between consenting adults ([sixteen] or over for Rhode Island, [eighteen] or over for New Jersey) is not a criminal offense, though marriage is not allowed in either state.[90]

I don't believe there are any other examples of incest in the New Testament. As we have just been made aware, there's a lack of consensus by the states as to whether this act is considered criminal. However, what we do know is that every state has concluded that anyone involved in such a relationship is not allowed to get married. And furthermore, scripturally speaking, any incestual sexual relationship would be classified as committing fornication.

So, how should we as Christians regard incest? I believe it should be regarded by us as a behavior that is not condoned.

Are there any other Scriptures that mention sexual relations with which Christians should not be involved?

Let's go forward to the book of 1 Corinthians.

1 Corinthians 6:9-11

> *Know ye not that the unrighteous shall not inherit the kingdom of God? Be not deceived: neither fornicators, nor idolaters, nor adulterers, nor effeminate, nor abusers of themselves with mankind, Nor thieves, nor covetous, nor drunkards, nor revilers, nor extortioners, shall inherit the kingdom of God. And such were some of you: but ye are washed, but ye are sanctified, but ye are justified in the name of the Lord Jesus, and by the Spirit of our God.*

The Apostle Paul declares a truth, which is not a surprise according to the Christian faith, that the unrighteous (the unsaved) shall not inherit (enter into) the Kingdom of God. And for whatever reason, perhaps because at the time, certain sins were considered acceptable in society and even esteemed as a means to worship or to satisfy some false deity, anyone who would commit such would not enter into God's Kingdom. Some of the sins mentioned, which are sexual in the description, are as follows.

- Fornicators – Those who have sex outside of marriage.
- Adultery – Sex with someone who is not your husband or wife.
- Effeminate or the abusers of themselves with mankind - the passive and active partners ... in male homosexual [relations] (Barrett);[91] men who submit to or who practice homosexuality.[92]

And after he mentioned these various behaviors, he said to the believers at Corinth that such were some of their actions that they themselves were involved in, but at salvation, three things happened to them which changed their lives forever.

- They were washed.

They were baptized into the Christian faith, being identified with Christ in His death and burial, which separated them from sin's power; and having been identified with Him in His resurrection, they became new creations walking in newness of life by the same power that raised Him from the dead.

- They were sanctified.

They were separated from common, earthly, or sinful uses, to be wholly employed in the service of the true God.[93]

- They were justified.

They were accepted as righteous by having entered into a new relationship with God.

And now that they were born-again, they had a new standing before God and the opportunity by means of the Word and the ministry of the Holy Spirit to no longer continue in these actions. So, these Scriptures further confirm that a Christian should not be involved with fornication, adultery, and homosexuality.

The next sexual practice we'll consider took place at what was called the temple of Aphrodite. I'm sure you could make an educated guess as to what I'm talking about. This is found in the book of 1 Corinthians.

. . .

1 Corinthians 6:15

> *Know ye not that your bodies are the members of Christ? shall I then take the members of Christ, and make them the members of an harlot? God forbid.*

Evidently, there were some believers at the church of Corinth who was engaging in sex with prostitutes. At one temple alone, called the temple of Aphrodite, there were said to be over 1,000 female prostitutes working there. The Apostle Paul's response to this was to remind them that their spiritual connection with Christ belongs not merely to the [soul] but also to the [body] so that [we're] flesh of His flesh.[94] He then said to them, shall I take a member (a part of Christ in vital union with him[95]) and engage this same body with a harlot (prostitute) and not affect my spiritual condition? He emphatically concluded his remarks by saying, *God forbid* (let it not be so). This verse clearly tells us that prostitution is not a sexual avenue that a Christian should be participating in.

We have one more Scripture section to look at, which will address a sexual practice that was mentioned in the article on Roman Sexual Morality but not elaborated on. Do you have any idea as to what sexual practice this is? Please stay in 1 Corinthians.

1 Corinthians 6:9

> *Know ye not that the unrighteous shall not inherit the kingdom of God? Be not deceived: neither fornicators, nor idolaters, nor adulterers, nor effeminate, nor abusers of themselves with mankind,*

There are some examples of this sexual practice in the Old Testament Scriptures. In the article on Roman Sexual Morality that we looked at in an earlier chapter, we found that this action was considered as being generally acceptable during Roman times, especially when committed on those who were of a lower social class. Do you remember what sexual practice this referred to?

The sexual practice we're talking about is called rape. In today's society, this word can mean sexual assault, forced stripping, or forced public nakedness. The online dictionary describes rape as unlawful sexual intercourse or any other sexual penetration of the vagina, anus, or mouth of another person, with or without force, by a sex organ, other body [parts], or foreign object, without the consent of the victim.[96]

While I couldn't find a storied example of such in the New Testament, some scholars believe that the Greek words *arsenokoitai* (abusers of themselves with mankind) and *malakoi* (effeminate) in 1 Corinthians 6:9 are specifically speaking out against these predatory practices of sexual abuse where a dominant, high-status man (viewed as masculine by patriarchal society) would sexually abuse a young boy or slave (seen as "effeminate" because of their lesser power in their patriarchal society[97]). Based on the acceptability of this action at this time, it would seem plausible that these two words, besides implying the sexual practice of pedophilia, could also refer to the predatory sexual abuse known as rape.

Scripture certainly has helped us in learning about what sexual practices God condones and which ones He does not. And so, here are the summarized findings.

1. Christians that are married and/or those who remain celibate can be a part of God's plan.
2. Marriage between a man and a woman is encouraged, especially if there's a desire to engage in sexual relations.
3. Fornication (having sex outside of marriage), lesbianism or homosexuality (sex with someone of the same gender), incest (sex with someone of the immediate or extended family), adultery (sex with someone other than one's husband or wife), prostitution (sex with someone who sells

> their body for pleasure), rape (forcible sexual assault), pedophilia (sex with a child), and polygamy (having more than one wife) are considered as actions that are not condoned by God.

After reading this summary, you might respond by saying, doesn't God support a loving relationship between two people? If you are talking about Christians who are married, male and female, the answer is yes.

What unbelievers do with their bodies in any realm, who operate in their sin nature, is considered works of the flesh. Some works are considered good or moral, while others are considered immoral or sinful. This is determined by societal norms. Neither work has any redemptive qualities in God's eyes. God's desire for them is that they get saved and learn how to walk in their new nature.

Let me say this another way as pertaining to the perception that God supports a loving relationship between two people. Having sexual *eros* relationships between two people, who are not saved, you could say, is like any other *eros* relationship involving two people who are not saved. They will love each other with *eros* love, but not God's *agape* love. So, with two unbelievers, or even believers who are operating in *eros* love is not the same as two believers operating in *agape* love. Operating in *eros* love is operating in the sin nature. Operating in *agape* love is walking in the new divine nature.

So, I believe this answers the comment made by a member of the Christian megachurch when he said, any relationship that I have with a man is part of God's plan and that it would be full of love, equal to any other.[98] *What we have learned is that neither is this eros type of love a part of God's plan, and neither is it full of love equal to God's agape love between two Christians.*

When there's a lack of clear teaching from the pulpit on any biblical topic or issue, then there will be confusion as to what the Word of God says about it. This will result in human perception based on societal norms becoming the standard for the members of a church to adhere to.

There are many Christians, like me at one time, whose sin nature continued to rule their lives after salvation. Whatever inclinations, passions, or propensities they gravitated toward before they were saved, they were still gravitating toward after they were saved. With these thoughts in mind, here's the million-dollar question.

How do Christians learn how to no longer be in subjection to the cravings and desires of their flesh (sin nature)?

As I was preparing to talk about this in the next chapter, something happened which changed my mind. It had to do with another comment that I heard while watching TV. It was by a different Christian male who apparently was running for the highest political office in the land. He mentioned that he was married to another male. But this was not the end of this proclamation. He added that he felt justified as a Christian to have made this decision before God for a particular reason.

In the next chapter, let's take a look at what the reason was that he believed caused his decision to be sanctioned by God and see if Scripture supported his claims. After we take a look at this, we'll attempt to answer the question posed beforehand. How does a Christian learn how to no longer be in subjection to the cravings and desires of his/her flesh?

8

GOD MADE ME LIKE THIS

As I was working on this study, I took a break and turned on my favorite morning news station. The panel had a guest who claimed to be a Christian and disclosed that he was married to someone of the same gender. *He went on to say something like, if anyone has an issue with this, then go to God because He made me like this.* This resonated with me in the sense that this statement sounded right, and I'm sure those that listened to it agreed, but I've learned over the years that Scripture should give us the answers to any question or comment that has any connection to do with God. *So, let's see if what was said is indeed supported by God's Word.*

Many of us are familiar with the Genesis story of Adam and Eve. Let's begin by going to this book.

Genesis 2:7

> *And the Lord God formed man of the dust of the ground, and breathed into his nostrils the breath of life; and man became a living soul.*

God made Adam's body from the dust of the ground. I wouldn't even begin to try to figure that out. And then it says He breathed into his nostrils the breath of life, and he became a living soul. The word *breath* refers to the breath that causes man to live, or in other words, it was the breath from God that caused Adam to live or become a living soul (a living creature).

But there's something else that God did to man when He made him.

Do you know what this was?

Genesis 1:26a

> *And God said, Let us make man in our image, after our likeness:...*

He made man after His image and likeness. The word *image* conveys to us the nature of Adam's soul in that it was not corrupt, and as to its moral disposition, it could be otherwise called original righteousness. The soul of Adam was created in the moral image of God, in knowledge, righteousness, and true holiness.[99]

> *Genesis 3:8a And they heard the voice of the Lord God walking in the garden in the cool of the day:*

After Eve was made from Adam's rib, we're told that both of them were placed in a geographical location called the Garden of Eden, where Scripture suggests they communicated with God and subsequently shared in His wisdom, love, truth, etc. Along with this, we're also told that they were made in the likeness of God. This word *likeness* refers back to the word *image* and describes it as being a resemblance in any quality, internal or external. So, as Adam and Eve responded to God's communication inwardly, they revealed His characteristics outwardly in their bodies.

Are there any other verses that give us more insight into man's nature at the time when he was first created?

Yes, there is. Further information is found in the book of Ecclesiastes.

Ecclesiastes 7:29

> Lo, *this only have I found, that God hath made man upright; but they have sought out many inventions.*

This verse tells us that God, as the creator of human life, made man upright. The word *upright* means that he was possessed of [the] ability to choose and follow what was just and right.[100] How did Adam know what was just and right? He knew what was just and right because he communicated with the one God who was, is, and always will be just and right in the Garden of Eden.

Did man remain upright, or in other words, did he remain made in God's image?

To answer this, we must go back to the sad story that took place after Adam and Eve were placed in the Garden of Eden, which tells us that both of them were instructed not to eat from one particular tree in the Garden called the Tree of Knowledge of Good and Evil. What we have come to learn is that an angel, who we now know was the Devil, was also on the earth at this time in the exact geographical location with the purpose of causing one or both of them to disobey God's command. Through his cunning, he deceived Eve into eating from this tree. She, in turn, convinced her husband also to eat from it.

As a result of their disobedience, there was one major impact that would affect all of their descendants. Do you know what this was?

Romans 5:12

Wherefore, as by one man sin entered into the world, and death by sin; and so death passed upon all men, for that all have sinned:

By one man, Adam, sin (human depravity) entered into the world. In other words, every human being born after that fateful decision would have a fallen nature passed onto them. Therefore, the uncorrupt moral disposition that characterized Adam and Eve's original nature became corrupted with a nature that sins.

Genesis 5:3 And Adam lived an hundred and thirty years, and begat a son in his own likeness, after his image; and called his name Seth:

And thus, mankind was no longer made in God's image but after the image of Adam, which is a morally depraved image. While his son would be born with the likeness (outward features) of his father and mother, his soul would be subject to moral disorder. And subsequently, a person's sinful character would be formed and described in the following manner according to Webster's dictionary. The peculiar qualities, impressed by nature or habit on a person, which distinguish him from others; these constitute real character, and the qualities which he is supposed to [possess] constitute his estimated [character] or reputation. [Hence,] we say, a character is not [formed] when the person has not acquired stable and distinctive qualities.[101]

However, some may argue that every human being is still made in the image of God at birth. Is this true? Please go to the book of Colossians, and we'll find out.

Colossians 3:10

And have put on the new man, which is renewed in knowledge after the image of him that created him:

The words *of him that created him* are to be taken as an analogy of the spiritual man or born-again Christian to Adam in the Garden of Eden before the fall. As Adam was created in God's image so the new man, the new creation, the Christian at the new birth, was recreated in God's image.

So, to say that God initially created mankind in body and soul after His image and likeness is correct. *To say that the nature that I now possess, along with its propensities and inclinations, is from God is incorrect. Therefore, the insinuation by the person running for political office that God made him gay is unscriptural. However, what we can say is true in this sense is that the whole universe of things was made by Christ. And all created beings are without independent existence apart from God.*

Some insinuate that there are other verses that support the conjecture that God made them in whatever way their actions indicate. Let's begin by going to the book of Psalms.

Psalms 100:3

> *Know ye that the LORD he is God: it is he that hath made us, and not we ourselves; we are his people, and the sheep of his pasture.*

This verse talks about the Jews who *Know* (to know by experience) *that the Lord (Yahweh) he is* (the one true) *God.* We're then told that *Yahweh* made them and not they themselves. This means that "Jehovah constituted us as a nation, His chosen people,"[102], *and not we ourselves* (how altogether of God's grace, not of our working even in part[103]).

As we can clearly see, these verses don't pertain to *Yahweh,* making each of those who are members of the Jewish nation in a certain actionable way. The next verse that we'll look at tells us that God created a nation of people whom He would mold into a certain form.

Isaiah 43:1

But now thus saith the Lord that created thee, O Jacob, and he that formed thee, O Israel, Fear not: for I have redeemed thee, I have called thee by thy name; thou art mine.

The book of Isaiah embraces all that was seen during the reigns of Uzziah, Jotham, Ahaz, and [Hezekiah,] that is, during the whole prophetic life of the prophet.[104] This includes the whole collection of prophecies delivered in the course of his ministry.[105] In this instance, he is communicating the thoughts of the Lord to the children of Israel who are currently under captivity to Babylon.

They are reminded by God that He *created* (brought them into existence) and *formed* (to mold into a form) them. In order to mold someone into a certain form, they would need to believe in the one who desires for changes to take place in their life and subsequently obey his instructions as delineated in the Mosaic Law.

The psalmist also assured them that they had nothing to fear. Their God will see to it that they will be *redeemed* (ransomed by means of a price) from their captivity and restored again to their homeland. The price will be the destruction of Babylon in the place of the ransomed captives.

Those who claim that God made them a certain way believe that their perspective is supported by the verses found in Psalms 139.

Psalms 139:13-14

13 For thou hast possessed my reins: thou hast covered me in my mother's womb.
14 I will praise thee; for I am fearfully and wonderfully made: marvellous are thy works; and that my soul knoweth right well.

This psalm has been attributed to King David. However, there are certain aspects that appear to indicate that it was written by someone else either during the Babylonian Captivity or after it ended. "In the first twelve verses of this [psalm] the author celebrates God's perfect knowledge of man's thoughts and actions; and the reason of this wonderful knowledge, namely, that God is the Maker of man.[106] Now, let's take a look at these verses.

This person goes on to say that God *hast possessed* (owned; created) *my reins* (kidneys; the whole body; conscience; personality; inward parts). There it is. What meaning should be used when talking about this persons' reins? I would say that it depends on the context or what do the other verses that accompany it talk about.

He goes on to say that God has *covered* (woven) him in his *mother's womb*. The word woven means that God had put his parts together, as one who weaves cloth or who makes a basket.[107] With this additional insight, we could suggest that the word *reins* refer to either the whole body and/or the inward parts.

However, he that said God made him in a particular way would say that God has possessed (created) his *reins* (his personality).

This appears to be a possible conclusion, but unfortunately, it doesn't take into account certain things. One of which is that the person who wrote this psalm was not only Jewish but someone who believed in *Yahweh* as He revealed Himself to him as his ancestor Abraham.

Romans 4:1-3

> *1 What shall we say then that Abraham our father, as pertaining to the flesh, hath found?*
> *2 For if Abraham were justified by works, he hath whereof to glory; but not before God.*
> *3 For what saith the scripture? Abraham believed God, and it was counted unto him for righteousness.*

Abraham, as to what he achieved by his flesh (circumcision), was found not to be justified (declared righteous; accepted as righteous) by his works (his own efforts). However, because he believed God (of trust in and acceptance of God's blessings[108]; of his unwavering assurance that what God had promised he would perform[109], i.e., that he would be a father of many nations; that his posterity should be like the stars of heaven[110], and that unto him and his descendants would be given land for an inheritance), it was counted unto him (put to his account; credited to his account) righteousness (to regard and treat him in connection with this as a righteous man; as one who was admitted to the favor and friendship of God[111]; a seal of righteousness was put on him).

Abraham, at one time, was an unbeliever whose sin nature characterized his thinking, speaking, and actions. And at some point in time, he believed in what God declared to him and subsequently in Him as the one true God. This caused him to become a new person, one who had become a friend of His. So, with these thoughts in mind, we could say that the Lord *possessed* (owned; created) his *reins* (his personality).

What this suggests is that the psalmist's personality was owned and thus created by *Yahweh* through cultivation and development by means of many areas such as obedience in following the godly instructions given by Israel's leaders along with adherence to the tenets of the Mosaic Law. This tells us that the psalmist's new personality was formed by the appropriation of divinely instituted principles.

We could conclude that at birth, sin or the sin nature is passed on. However, when someone believes in *Yahweh* in the Old Testament or repents to God the Father and believes in His Son in the New Testament, they become a new person whose new personality is developed as they appropriate God's perspective for spiritual growth.

Now that we know what sexual practices are condoned by God and which ones are not, along with the fact that all of us have a sin nature that has inclinations and passions in many areas, especially in the sexual realm, which is the result of the fall of Adam and Eve in the Garden of Eden, we have a significant question before us. How do we as Christians learn how to no longer be in subjection to the cravings and desires of our flesh? We'll find this out in the next chapter.

9

HOW DO CHRISTIANS LEARN TO NO LONGER BE IN SUBJECTION TO THE CRAVINGS AND DESIRES OF THEIR FLESH?

The person we had been referencing in the article had some spiritual avenues at his disposal. In my hometown, every so often, on a Saturday night on GOD TV, there would be a broadcast of worship, praise, and teaching service from the same church that this person was affiliated with. The staging area would be set up for many musicians to perform. The words from the songs were uplifting and impactful. In some cases, this was followed by a guest speaker, each of whom had a message that was unique and anointed. And then there was the presentation of the gospel to which many unbelievers responded.

I'm unaware of what else was going on for the rest of the week in the church assembly. In this instance, I would assume there were some outreaches and other worship, praise, and teaching services held throughout the week. Might there possibly be Bible studies available? So, here is my point. I have to believe that this church also had its own people in leadership to teach on the various doctrines of the faith, i.e., eternal security, redemption, sanctification, giving financially, eternal rewards, etc.

. . .

And besides learning about the tenets of the Christian faith, what else is extremely important is learning how to address the weaknesses and strengths of our sin nature.

It appears that this might have been attempted to be handled according to some of the declarations from the article entitled, "Sex Abuse & Gay Conversion Therapy: The Dark Past of Justin Bieber's Megachurch Hillsong" that we have mentioned on a couple of occasions. Here is some of what was said in relation to addressing gay behavior. Alex, a former member of this church, quit after a traumatic coming out where he said he was referred to his youth pastor to counseling that proposed to make him straight – the kind of conversion we now know is based on pseudoscience.[112]

I have never heard of pseudoscience, but what I do know is at salvation, we're made new creatures. However, the experiential realization of this positional reality (as God sees us as being a finished product) is a process. I admit that trying to grasp this and see it coming to fruition in our own lives is mysterious and painful at times. After I got saved, I still attended nightclubs, got drunk, looked for girls, said swear words, smoked cigarettes, had violent tendencies, harbored impure thoughts about others, had fears of speaking in front of people, had pornographic inclinations, and had a very bad view of myself. But the one thing I knew beyond a shadow of doubt was that God had come into my life! However, in my experience, I was an extreme mess.

How could I possibly learn how to be an overcomer in all or any of these areas of weakness?

Like this fellow believer, God provided me with spiritual guidance to attend a particular church, which likewise had a music ministry along with worship, praise, and teaching at least three times a week. It was connected to a headquarters facility located not too far away from the branch ministry I was attending. The headquarters provided live radio broadcasts Monday through Friday, varying educational degrees in Christian ministry, street witnessing outreach, a monthly newsletter, and if a branch church put in a request for a guest speaker, usually this would be granted. I loved this church. The teachings were anointed with God's saturating presence. I was learning about my new faith. But I still had issues with the inclinations and passions of my sin nature. Old ways of thinking, feeling, speaking, and in some cases, acting remained the same. I needed a heavenly life raft.

Then, one day something dawned on me. As I listened to the pastor of the branch ministry speak, one thing that resonated with me was his expansive knowledge about who he was in Christ, as evidenced in his command of bringing forth pertinent Scripture after Scripture from his tongue without looking in the Bible. And there it was all along. The solution for my many issues was to learn, memorize, meditate, and apply God's Word concerning each and every area of weakness of my sin nature.

And along with this, there was something else I had learned. Whenever I thought about myself, others, or the circumstances of life from a human perspective, I would lose the presence of God permeating my life. There were many times when I would hear anointed music and messages under the power of the Holy Spirit, and I was unable to be impacted by His individual and corporate ministry because I was operating in the wrong mindset. The following verses illustrate this perfectly.

Romans 8:5-6

> *5 For they that are after the flesh do mind the things of the flesh; but they that are after the Spirit the things of the Spirit. For to be carnally minded is death; but to be spiritually minded is life and peace.*

What this tells us [is] that they who live under the influences of the corrupt and sinful desires[113] of the sin nature are characterized as being carnally minded, and as such, they focus their thoughts on what their body wants. On the other hand, those who live after the Holy

Spirit think about what the Spirit wants, and as [such,] their mind is controlled or dominated by[114] Him.

> *6 For to be carnally minded is death; but to be spiritually minded is life and peace.*

With these thoughts in mind, we can conclude that if we're carnally minded, i.e., think only about what [our] body wants,[115] we'll experience misery and condemnation. However, if we're spiritually minded, i.e., making His thoughts the object of the mind, the end and aim of the actions, to cultivate the graces of the Spirit, and to submit to His influence; ... to seek those feelings and views which the Holy Spirit produces, and to follow His leadings,[116] we'll experience life (eternal resurrection life; the only path of happiness[117]) and peace [repose (state of being at rest) and true bliss[118]].

All this sounds great, but how do we cultivate the influences of the Spirit?

We cultivate His influences by making them the object of our minds. You might be thinking you have some idea of what I mean, but not really. That's okay. This idea of cultivating the Spirit's graces is easy to say but not necessarily easy to understand.

In respect to the question at hand, how does a Christian learn how to no longer be in subjection to the cravings and desires of their flesh? Which grace of the Spirit do you think will help us in this endeavor?

There are nine graces of the Spirit per the book of Galatians. Any guesses?

Galatians 5:22-23

> *But the fruit of the Spirit is love, joy, peace, longsuffering,*

> *gentleness, goodness, faith, Meekness, temperance: against such there is no law.*

The fruit of the Spirit that will help us is temperance. What is temperance? Temperance means being able to say no to one's desires.[119] It also means to have mastery over one's desires and impulses.[120] Did you hear that? God's Word says we can have mastery over our desires and impulses, that is, if we want to have mastery over them.

If you keep on referring to yourself by saying, oh, God can't change me. I'm a lying Christian; I'm a fornicating Christian; I'm an adulterous Christian; I'm a gay Christian; etc., and I will never change, then you won't. You will be a new person in Christ, living as the old person you used to be. Is this how you want to continue to live as a son or daughter of God? If you are not sure whether this is what is going on in your life, then ask yourself these questions.

Do you proclaim that Jesus has changed your life, and yet you exhibit no changes in your behavior?

Do you proclaim that Jesus has changed your life, and yet you express to others, believers and unbelievers, that He condones certain sinful sexual actions?

If the answers are yes and yes, then this question remains to be answered.

Do you really want to exhibit Christ-likeness to others?

What is Christ-likeness?

Christ-likeness is operating in the fruit of the Spirit and exhibiting the characteristics of these nine elements toward others while amidst the circumstances of life.

Where you are at right now is where I was years ago in my walk with God, at a crossroads. Do I continue to live to gratify the sinful desires of my sin nature, or do I make the necessary decisions to cultivate the fruit of the Spirit in my life? I hope your answer is the latter. If it is, then what I'm going to present to you next is what I believe will help you to cultivate the spiritual grace called temperance.

While it's true that we should learn how to cultivate each of the nine elements, we need to work on them one at a time. And with respect to this study, temperance will be the one we'll focus on. Are you ready to embark on making certain decisions that will help you be an overcomer in the area of *eros* sexual desires or propensities? If so, the next chapter will reveal how to do this.

10

HOW DO WE CULTIVATE THE SPIRITUAL GRACE CALLED TEMPERANCE SO THAT WE WILL BECAME AN OVERCOMER IN THE AREA OF EROS SEXUAL DESIRES?

In order to develop mastery over our sexual desires, the following divine prescriptions are available for you to cultivate. Are you ready to find out what these are and how to apply them to your spiritual life?

CHANGING THOUGHTS ABOUT MYSELF

You need to start thinking about yourself as God sees you and as you really are as a son or daughter of Him. Below are some of the verses you should memorize and speak out loud to yourself when you wake up in the morning. I have presented each verse as it appears in the King James Version of the Bible and the same verse again, albeit with some additional meanings from the Koine Greek that might provide a more down-to-earth understanding of it. My advice is for you to memorize the main verse and pray to God the Father for guidance in the name of the Son by means of the ministry of the Holy Spirit in appropriating whatever else will help you in cultivating the spiritual quality of temperance.

> *Colossians 3:10 And have put on the new man, which is*

renewed in knowledge after the image of him that created him:

Colossians 3:10 And have put on the new man (the person who we're now in Christ)*, which is renewed* (a new character in the course of formation) *in knowledge* (to know oneself in the light of God) *after the image of him* (so as to resemble Christ; the renewal process has as its goal the complete restoration in the creature of the likeness of the creator[121]) *that created him:*

2 Corinthians 5:17 Therefore if any man be in Christ, he is a new creature: old things are passed away; behold, all things are become new.

2 Corinthians 5:17 Therefore if any man be in Christ, he is a new creature (a new creation; a new being; the new person on the inside[122])*: old things* (things that characterized the pre-Christian life[123]) *are passed away* (have disappeared; are finished and gone)*; behold, all things are become new* (the whole sphere of being; which God himself owns as his workmanship, and which He can look on and pronounce very good[124]).

Ephesians 4:22 That ye put off concerning the former conversation the old man, which is corrupt according to the deceitful lusts;
23 And be renewed in the spirit of your mind;
24 And that ye put on the new man, which after God is created in righteousness and true holiness.

Ephesians 4:22 That ye put off (put away) *concerning the former conversation* (manner of life; behavior) *the old man* (the unsaved person dominated by the totally depraved nature[125]), *which is corrupt* (morally decaying) *according to the deceitful lusts* (lusts excited by deceit, i.e., by deceitful influences seducing to sin)[126]

23 *And be renewed* (to be renovated by inward reformation) *in the spirit of your mind* (by the Holy Spirit united with your spirit, and influencing your mind;[127] intellectual and spiritual renewal; as the mind understands the truth of God's Word, [it's] gradually transformed by the Spirit, and this renewal leads to a changed life[128]);

24 *And that ye put on* (choose to put on) *the new man* (the brand-new man; the new person), *which after God* (after the pattern God, the new birth, the new life in Christ[129]) *is created in righteousness and true holiness* (causes everyone to see that you are living according to God's truth[130]).

Colossians 2:10 And ye are complete in him, which is the head of all principality and power:

Colossians 2:10 And ye are complete (to fully possess a maximum amount of blessing, i.e., to be richly furnished with the power and gifts of the Holy Spirit[131]) *in him, which is the head of all principality and power:*

Ephesians 1:7 In whom we have redemption through his blood, the forgiveness of sins, according to the riches of his grace;

Ephesians 1:7 In whom we have redemption (deliverance effected through the death of Christ from the retributive wrath of a holy God and the merited penalty of sin[132]) *through his blood* (the price paid to

> divine justice), *the forgiveness of sins* (to throw a person's sins behind one's back; not to remember any longer a person's sins), *according to the riches of his grace;*

You might say, well, what if I decide to start to memorize some of the Scriptures mentioned and begin to think differently about myself? How will I be benefitted? Do you know that Scripture tells us what will happen if we decide to appropriate God's truths about ourselves?

Please go to the book of 1 John.

1 John 2:5

> *But whoso keepeth his word, in him verily is the love of God perfected: hereby know we that we are in him.*

This verse tells us that whosoever keeps (keeps on continually keeping) His Word (all that He has made known to us as His will in regard to our conduct), the love of God will be perfected (produced in us by the Holy Spirit and as such we'll be characterized, not by any representative trait or quality of his [our] own personality, but merely as the subject of the work of divine love[133]). Did you get what was just said? I will rephrase it. If you habitually keep God's Word, you will no longer be characterized by any representative trait (behavior that could involve sexual tendencies ascribing to self-benefit, self-gratification, etc.) of your personality, but of *agape* love, i.e., a self-less, self-sacrificial love toward others for their physical and spiritual well-being.

Now that we know how we should start out each day in the morning, what else can help us in becoming an overcomer in the area of *eros* sexual inclinations or propensities of the sin nature?

CONFESSING MY SINS – THE MANY BENEFITS OF SUCH

You might say, you have got to be kidding me. I learned about this in catechism, and I'm not going to go to someone and tell them about my faults. Well, I have good news for you. From what I have learned in Scripture, we have the privilege to go directly to God the Father when we sin, whether it be in our thoughts, words, or actions.

Ephesians 2:18

> *For through him we both have access by one Spirit unto the Father.*

We have direct access to God the Father by means of the Holy Spirit, whom we received at salvation.

As I told you earlier, after I got saved, I thought, spoke, and still did things as an unbeliever. I knew God had changed me, but that's all I knew. When I began to learn about the doctrines of the faith, especially what thoughts, words, and actions were considered sinful, I realized how many more of my thoughts were corrupted. How was I to address these continual thoughts of sinful imprisonment? By confessing them to God the Father.

Herein lies the problem. If we don't think about ourselves, others, and the circumstances of life differently, we'll never come out from under the misery of the soul due to sin. So, what is the remedy? The remedy is learning and meditating on a different perspective other than our own, i.e., learning and meditating on God's perspective, His Word.

Many Christians who are encouraged to confess their sins don't, why not? They don't think they have to because they would argue that all of their sins were forgiven at the cross. Is this true? It's true that all our sins were forgiven at the cross, but it's not true that we don't have to confess our sins. What is the purpose and benefit of confessing our sins?

Please go to the book of 1 John.

1 John 1:9

If we confess our sins, he is faithful and just to forgive us our sins, and to cleanse us from all unrighteousness.

The word *confess* can have different meanings. One, it could mean to admit or declare oneself guilty of what one is accused of. There will be times when we're approached by an unbeliever or believer about something we have said or done against them, where if true, we should confess our guilt to them and God the Father. In other instances, we might have said or done something to someone else and realized later on that we committed a fault. Likewise, we should go to the person offended and make [a] confession to our [fellow men] of offenses against them.[134] Second, this word could also mean to have any sin in our life discovered for us by the Holy Spirit, and ever eager to confess it and put it out of the life by the power of that same Holy Spirit[135]). When God the Holy Spirit brings us awareness in our minds of sin, then confess it to God the Father, and after you have done so, don't look back (don't think about it again).

Now that we know what the conditions are for confessing sin, what is the purpose and benefit of doing such?

We find the answer to this question in the word *forgive*. One definition of this word in response to our confession of sin is that discipline (chastisement) is removed from God the Father. What is chastisement? Chastisement refers to some sort of divine discipline that might involve physical sickness. So, confession of sin can bring about forgiveness from God that turns discipline into a blessing. What kind of blessing? The blessing of being restored back to fellowship with God the Father that was broken by that sin.[136] And, by the way, fellowship also can be referred to as recovering the filling of the Spirit. What does it mean to be filled with the Spirit? We have already studied this, but it's good to take another look at it.

Please turn your Bible, if you have it handy, to the book of Ephesians.

Ephesians 5:18

> *And be not drunk with wine, wherein is excess; but be filled with the Spirit.*

The word *filled* refers to the believer being under the Spirit's control. It also suggests the idea that this condition occurs because the believer has yielded themselves to Him. And when we're yielded to Him, He is said to control us in our mind, emotions, and will.[137] Because of such, He will be filling (furnishing; supplying) us with Himself, which is another way of saying that when this spiritual condition takes place, we'll experience His presence (divine joy; divine peace) in our lives.

As we can see, confession of sin can bring about many benefits for us. It turns discipline from God into blessing. It restores us to fellowship with God the Father. And it recovers the filling of the Holy Spirit, whereby we're able once again to experience His presence. So, if you are thinking about yourself in a different way and are confessing your sins to God the Father and/or to someone whom you may have offended, you should begin to notice glimpses of the Spirit's involvement in your life.

The next thing that inhibits a believer from going forward in the plan of God has to do with something that I think most believers are not mindful of. While this is extremely important, for some reason, other things seem to take precedence over it. It's probably something that will surprise you.

THE ANOINTING BREAKS THE YOKE

What am I referring to here? Let's begin by taking a look at an example of such from the book of Isaiah.

. . .

Isaiah 10:27

> *And it shall come to pass in that day, that his burden shall be taken away from off thy shoulder, and his yoke from off thy neck, and the yoke shall be destroyed because of the anointing.*

The Assyrian army has invaded Judah and has as its goal to conquer its capital city, Jerusalem. However, the yoke [(the oppression and calamity[138] (adversity)] of the Assyrians shall be taken away by God, who will give a word to the prophet Isaiah that will provide confidence to their king, King Hezekiah of Judah that He will provide deliverance through His own intervention. As those anointed, the prophet Isaiah and Hezekiah relied on their God; He, in turn, went into the camp of the Assyrians and killed 145,000 of their army.

The king of Assyria, Sennacherib, seeing the killing fields of his army before his eyes, turned from his intended plan with however many soldiers he had left alive and returned back to the capital city of Assyria, called Nineveh. When he arrived there, instead of contemplating that maybe--just maybe--what had taken place was a miraculous intervention by the God of the Jews, as usual, he entered into the house of his god named Nisroch where two of his own sons were waiting to kill him with the sword, which they did.

What we could say about this anointing is that it's a type of our deliverance when we choose to obey God's Word in the power of the Spirit. Deliverance from what? Deliverance from whatever is causing oppression, i.e., from whatever we have been focusing on, which are those fleshy sexual lusts or passions that try to overwhelm us with their intentions for fulfillment through various *eros* forms of sexual activity.

Let's take another look at this word *anointing* as it appears again, this time in a New Testament book called 1 John.

. . .

1 John 2:27

> *But the anointing which ye have received of him abideth in you, and ye need not that any man teach you: but as the same anointing teacheth you of all things, and is truth, and is no lie, and even as it hath taught you, ye shall abide in him.*

But the anointing, the person of the Holy Spirit, which you have received of Christ, abides (has taken up permanent residency) in you. *And you need not that any man teach you,* meaning *that no teacher, even a God-appointed one, is the only and ultimate source of the saint's instruction.*[139] The same anointing teaches you all things (under the guidance of the Spirit you must test the teaching of men as you search the Bible for yourself (cf. Acts 17:11);[140] as he endues us with judgment and discernment, lest we should be deceived by lies[141]).

So, the anointing is the person of the Holy Spirit. Not only does He impact us with His presence, but He provides us with discernment when we're listening to someone who proclaims they are presenting godly instruction.

What are some of the truths that we should be aware of which comprise godly doctrine?

- That there's one God, who evidences Himself in three persons, otherwise known as the Trinity, with each person being deity.
- That salvation is only in one person, Jesus Christ, who is deity (contains the same divine essence as God the Father and God the Holy Spirit).
- That a person is saved by repenting to God the Father for their sins and believing in His Son, Jesus Christ.
- That there's no other way to receive the Holy Spirit, become a child of God, and have the assurance of eternal life but by repentance and belief.
- That in order to be filled with the Spirit, we need to confess

known sin and recover (reflect upon God's Word with respect to ourselves, others, and the circumstances of life).

These are some of the truths we should hear about when receiving instruction from those in leadership. Otherwise, in all likelihood, those in the assembly won't have received the indwelling Spirit and subsequently won't grow spiritually. Sadly, if this is not the case, then they and their leaders will be characterized like those mentioned in the book of 2 Timothy.

2 Timothy 3:5

Having a form of godliness, but denying the power thereof: from such turn away.

They will only have an outward appearance of godliness. However, by exhibiting sinful behavior like those who are not saved, it will be evident in their actions that they haven't changed. Throughout their life, character, and conversation, they gave the lie to their Christian profession. Christianity with them was an outward form.[142] Why was this the case? This was the case because they refused to allow access to their lives, the divine power that leads to salvation, along with the divine power provided by the Spirit that is inherent in godliness and operates upon souls. And according to Whom, [we're] instructed to have no kind of fellowship with them.[143] Keep in mind when attending a local assembly, the truths should be prevalent so that we're able to recognize that those in leadership and those who attend are saved and have received the indwelling Spirit will be made evident to us by Him who is the true teacher that will assist us in breaking the yoke of sexual inclinations and passions.

What else will help us in addressing our sinful tendencies and inclinations?

THINKING ABOUT OTHERS

Hopefully, if you have responded to the suggestions previously mentioned, you are in a better place spiritually. You are thinking differently about yourself. You are confessing mental, verbal, and overt sins to God the Father and to those you have offended. You are participating in a Spirit-filled assembly where God the Holy Spirit shows up and where you are learning how to be filled with His presence. And the next step is to learn more verses that will cause you to have the proper mindset toward believers and unbelievers with respect to how we should be thinking about them as relating to sexual inclinations and tendencies. Some of these verses are those which will follow.

We'll begin by looking at verses that pertain to what we should be thinking about concerning unbelievers.

> *Luke 19:10 For the Son of man is come to seek and to save that which was lost.*

> *Luke 19:10 For the Son of man is come* (as an application, because we're saved God can use us in this respect) *to seek and to save that which was lost* (people who have gone astray).

> *1 Peter 2:11 Dearly beloved, I beseech you as strangers and pilgrims, abstain from fleshly lusts, which war against the soul;*
>
> *12 Having your conversation honest among the Gentiles: that, whereas they speak against you as evildoers, they may by your good works, which they shall behold, glorify God in the day of visitation.*

> *1 Peter 2:11 Dearly beloved, I beseech you as strangers* (having a house in a city without the rights of citizenship) *and pilgrims* (staying for a time in a

foreign land), *abstain* (not only refraining from indulging in something but of not allowing it to dominate one's life) *from fleshly lusts* (bodily passions), *which war against* (are opposed to) *the soul* (that part of a person which can relate directly to God's Spirit[144]);
12 Having your conversation (behavior) *honest* (telling the truth: to do that which is right, beautiful by reason of purity of heart and life, and hence, praiseworthy; morally good, noble[145]) *among the Gentiles* (unbelievers)*: that, whereas they speak against you as evildoers, they may by your good works* (good deeds; works which, on careful consideration must move the pagan to praise God[146]), *which they shall behold* (look intently upon), *glorify God in the day of visitation.*

Likewise, how should we be thinking about fellow believers, and subsequently, what are our actions that we should be exhibiting before them and toward them?

1 Peter 1:22 Seeing ye have purified your souls in obeying the truth through the Spirit unto unfeigned love of the brethren, see that ye love one another with a pure heart fervently:

1 Peter 1:22 Seeing ye have purified (you have gotten rid of the sin that spoiled you[147]) *your souls in obeying the truth* (habitual obedience to the Word) *through the Spirit unto unfeigned* (some had put a mask of feigned love over their usual countenances when associating with certain others of their brethren[148]) *love* (brotherly love; the context in which [it's] found is concerned with one's attitude toward one's fellow Christian as contrasted to one's former worldly associates;[149] one likes another person because that person is like himself in the sense that that person reflects in his own personality the same characteristics, the same likes and dislikes that he himself has[150]) *of the brethren, see that ye love* (divine love) *one another with a pure* [not for the love of ourselves; to not use for our advantage; free from hypocrisy (a pretense of having a virtuous character[151])] *heart* (mind) *fervently* (in an all-out manner):

1 Timothy 4:12 Let no man despise thy youth; but be thou an example of the believers, in word, in conversation, in charity, in spirit, in faith, in purity.

1 Timothy 4:12 Let no man despise thy youth; but be thou an example (like Timothy our life should be an example; an example to be imitated; a model to be followed) *of the believers, in word* (in what we say privately and in publicly; in doctrine; teaching nothing but the truth of God[152]), *in conversation* (in the whole of conduct), *in charity* (in agape love; the motivation of our life is from God's love), *in spirit* (in the manner and disposition in which thou dost all things[153]), *in faith* (in faithfulness to Christ; in all trials show to believers by your example, how they ought to maintain unshaken confidence in God[154]), *in purity* (an upright and morally blameless life, and specifically as referring to being free from any immoral acts, especially acts related to sex[155]).

And there you have it. Our mindset is such that we have at the forefront of it sharing the gospel with unbelievers so they can receive the indwelling Spirit and embark on a new life of faith. And as for believers, we're operating toward them in *agape* love, a sacrificial love that has as its object the spiritual and physical benefit of someone else in mind.

The final decision that you will need to make that will enhance your spiritual growth is one that is not easy to make because it seems to be contrary to the *agape* love in which we desire to operate.

A FRIEND OF SINNERS

After I got saved, I wanted to tell everyone about my conversion to the Christian faith, and I did. Doors opened to preach the gospel. Some of my relatives and friends got saved. One of the difficulties I noticed early on was associating with some of my unsaved friends while professing to them that my life had changed. Their mindset was, hey, come on let's party. It was about going to church on Sunday and living like hell the rest of the week.

It's true that Jesus was criticized by the Pharisees for hanging around with sinners. But the difference between Him and me was that He was always Spirit-filled and spiritually mature. The unsaved didn't affect His sin nature because he didn't have one. His life affected others and not the other way around.

When we get saved, our sin nature is still very much in control. It takes time to learn how to think differently about ourselves, others, and the circumstances of life. We need a constant intake of the Word of God in the power of the Spirit before we begin to see small measurable spiritual changes in our lives. In the meantime, how do we address associating with our friends who are unsaved and continue to live in behavioral patterns that we had also come to accept and engage in ourselves before we were saved?

The best way to answer this is to be introspective concerning yourself as to what begins to happen in your thought processes, your speech, and actions when you hang around with some of them. What I mean is if they are encouraging you to think, speak, and act the way you were before you were saved, you have to make a decision concerning how much time you should be willing to spend with them. While the object of our faith should be to witness the gospel to them at some point, how would they even respond to it if our testimony is such that it's still reflective of the person we used to be and not the new person we have become in Christ?

I can only tell you from personal experience that the temptation to commit fornication, adultery, take drugs, etc., was too great for me when I hung around with certain friends whose orientation was continually toward such conduct. So, I decided to immerse myself in learning the Word, gathering together with the assembly of believers, volunteering in church activities, etc. While I initially did feel guilty in not contacting my former friends, I knew that the only way I would be a testimony for Christ toward them in the future would be to get to know Christ intimately first.

As some might say, all good things must come to an end, but in the case of this study, at least not yet. I would like to provide for you in the final chapter some articles on testimonies that are about maintaining continual victory over sinful sexual desires and actions.

11

TESTIMONIES ABOUT MAINTAINING CONTINUAL VICTORY OVER SEXUAL ABUSE AND SINFUL SEXUAL DESIRES

Thank God that our sinful inclinations and tendencies no more define us. In Christ, we're no longer who we used to be. By means of the Word of God and the power of the Holy Spirit, we can think anew and experience the anointing which breaks the yoke.

Learning how to walk in the Spirit and evidencing Christ-likeness in our words and actions is a process, a daily reflection by us as to the new truths that have been revealed to us and appropriated by us as soon as we wake up in the morning and meditate upon throughout our day. It's not deliverance from, but deliverance within. So, the admonition is for us to put on the new man, the new person we have become, and to set our affections (mind) on things above (heavenly realities and values) and not on things below (the former life and everything of an evil nature that pertained to it[156]). And if we do, we'll evidence a testimony of maintaining continual victory over sinful sexual desires like our fellow believers have been able to do so, whose stories are about to be presented in the articles that follow.

JOYCE MEYER OVERCAME ABUSE BY HER FATHER

Joyce Meyer, one of America's most prominent Christian speakers and authors, overcame sexual abuse by her father.

> "My father did rape me, numerous times, at least [two hundred] times," she told Charisma Magazine.

Meyer, a down-to-earth public speaker with a high-flying prosperity gospel ministry, finally broke years of silence in 2012 by revealing her childhood trauma. She decided she needed to share her testimony to help others suffering similar hurts.

> "I was sexually, mentally, [emotionally,] and verbally abused by my father as far back as I can remember until I left home at the age of [eighteen]," she said. "He did many terrible things...some [of] which are too distasteful for me to talk about publicly. But I want to share my testimony because so many people have been hurt, and they need to realize that someone has made it through their struggles."

Meyer grew up in St. Louis, [Missouri,] with a dad who "was born in the hills — way back in the hills. In his family, incest was just part of the culture," she told Charisma. At age [nine], she told her mother what [had] happened. But mom did nothing. When Meyer was [fourteen], her mom caught her dad in the act. But mom was emotionally incapable of confronting the situation and left instead.

In response to her trauma, Meyer accepted Jesus in a local church at age 9. But her mind was in a state of confusion. Shortly after graduating from high school, she married a part-time car salesman, who cheated on her and persuaded her to embezzle from her employer. After she divorced him, she married her current husband, Dave Meyer, an engineering draftsman in 1967, according to Wikipedia.

Then one day in [1976,] she was praying intensely while driving to work and heard God call her name. She describes what she felt as "liquid love" flowing from God. The emotional experience was the start of a closer walk with God that would bring her into ministry.

With a no-nonsense folksy style that ingratiated her with her audiences, Meyer rose quickly through the ministerial ranks in ever-larger churches until she resigned to launch her own ministry in 1985. "Life in the Word" began with broadcasts on six radio stations from Chicago to Kansas City. In 1993, she and her husband launched a television ministry.

Meanwhile, her book-writing ministry also prospered. Publishing house Hachette Book paid Meyer more than $10 million for the rights to her backlist catalog of independently released books in 2002, according to Wikipedia. On the outside, things were going well. On the inside, Meyer had to deal with the emotional scars from her childhood.

> "I was so profoundly ashamed because of this," Meyer said. "I was ashamed of me, and I was ashamed of my father and what he did. I was also constantly afraid. There was no place I ever felt safe growing up. I don't think we can even begin to imagine what kind of damage this does to a child.
>
> "At [school,] I pretended I had a normal life, but I felt lonely all the time and different from everyone else. I never felt like I fit in, and I wasn't allowed to participate in [after school] activities, go to sports events or [parties,] or date boys. Many [times,] I had to make up stories about why I couldn't do anything with my classmates. For so [long,] I lived with pretense and lies.
>
> "What I learned about love was actually perversion," she added. "My father told me what he did to me was

> special and because he loved me. He said everything he did was good, but it had to be our secret because no one else would [understand,] and it would cause problems in the family."

Meyer eventually reached a place in her life when she knew she had to forgive her father.

> "I'm happy to say that God gave me the grace completely, 100%, [to] forgive my father," she said in [a] YouTube video. "It took some time, but I was able to do it."

Then she had to share the horrifying story.

> "As long as I kept this secret, I couldn't get free from the pain of it," she said.

She explained her struggle with her dad and wants people to know that anyone that has been abused can recover if they will give their life completely to Jesus.

> "God didn't get me out of the situation when I was a child, but He did give me the strength to get through it," Meyer said. "It's true my father abused me and didn't love and protect me the way he should have, and at times it seemed no one would ever help [me,] and it would never end.
>
> "But God always had a plan for my life, and He has redeemed me. He has taken what Satan meant for harm and turned it into something good. He has taken away my shame and given me a double reward and recompense."

When her father was sick and dying on a hospital [bed,] he told her, "Joyce, [I'm] sorry you feel I hurt you. But I still don't understand what was so bad about what I did." It wasn't much as far as repentance went.

God told her that she was to move him close to her house and take care of him. Meyer's husband disagreed with the plan, but it soon was confirmed that God had spoken to her.

As God supplied the grace, she showed her father love [every day]. Every need he had, she attempted to meet. She bought his food and clothing.

One day he broke down in tears. He called Joyce and Dave to his bedside and fully repented: "[I'm] sorry for what I did to you. I have wanted to say this to you for a long time, but I didn't have the guts," he said. "Dave, [I'm] sorry for what I did to you. [I'm] sorry I hurt your wife. Please forgive me."

Meyer knelt beside [him] and led her father in the sinner's prayer. He then asked Meyer to baptize him. Meyer baptized her father on Dec. 2, [2001,] in front of hundreds of people at the Dream Center she founded in St. Louis' inner city. From a "mean snake," God had begun to transform him into a "sweet old man."

> "I know that I know that I know, that God has redeemed, and what Satan meant for bad God has turned to good," she said.[157]

FROM GAY TO GOSPEL: THE FASCINATING STORY OF BECKET COOK

Ten years ago, Becket Cook was a gay man in Hollywood who had achieved great success as a set designer in the fashion industry. He worked with stars and supermodels, from Natalie Portman to Claudia Schiffer, traveling the world to design [photoshoots] for the likes of

Vogue and Harper's Bazaar. He attended award shows and parties at the homes of Paris Hilton and Prince. He spent summers swimming in Drew Barrymore's pool. A decade later, Cook [had] moved on from that life—and he doesn't miss it.

What changed for Cook? He met Jesus. On a momentous day in September 2009, while drinking coffee with a friend at Intelligentsia in L.A.'s Silver Lake neighborhood, Cook started chatting with a group of young people sitting at a nearby table—physical Bibles opened in front of them (remember, this was 2009). They were from a church called Reality L.A. (where TGC Council member Jeremy Treat now serves as lead pastor), and they invited Cook to visit the church.

Cook took them up on the invitation and visited Reality L.A. the next Sunday, where he heard the gospel and gave his life to Jesus. He never looked back, trading his gay identity for a new identity in Christ. In the years since, Cook completed a degree at Talbot School of Theology and wrote a memoir of his conversion, *A Change of Affection: A Gay Man's Incredible Story of Redemption,* which just released.

I recently met up with Cook at Intelligentsia—the place where his encounter with coffee-drinking, Bible-studying Christians set his conversion in motion. Here is an edited transcript of our conversation.

Take me back to that day, in this very coffee shop, [ten] years ago. What was going on in your life that made the soil, so to speak, ready to receive the gospel seed?

> It was a moment in Paris six months earlier. I was at a fashion party and just felt empty: I had done everything in Hollywood, met everyone, traveled everywhere. [Yet,] I was overwhelmed with emptiness at this party. It was one of the most intense "is that all there is?" moments in my life. I had already been wrestling with questions about the

meaning of life, searching for it in all sorts of ways. But I knew God was never an [option] because I was gay. It was off the table. I wasn't confused about what the Bible had to say about homosexuality. I knew it was clear. But I was still searching for meaning.

[So,] when I came to this coffee shop six months later and saw that group of young people with their Bibles open, I started asking them questions. They explained the gospel, what they believed. I asked what their church believed about homosexuality, and they explained that they believed it [was] a sin. I appreciated their honesty and that they didn't beat around the bush. But the reason I was able to accept their answer was because I had that moment in Paris. Five years [earlier,] I would have been like, [you] guys are insane. You're in the dark ages. But [instead,] I was like, [maybe] I could be wrong. Maybe this actually is a sin. [So,] I was open to it in the moment. And then they invited me to church.

When you showed up to church that first Sunday at Reality, you ended up becoming a Christian. What happened?

Tim Chaddick preached the sermon that day, and everything he was saying basically turned what I knew about religion upside down. I grew up in Catholic schools, and I honestly thought religion was just being a good person, doing good things. I don't think the priests in my high school once explained what the gospel was. Not once. [So,] when Tim was preaching all these things that were the exact opposite of what I thought religion was, I was like, [whoa.] It all really resonated, and it prompted me to go forward at the end of the service to receive prayer. It was shocking and unexpected to me, a Road to Damascus moment. It was so powerful, so all-consuming. I was all-in.

What did discipleship look like for you after you got saved?

Tim and I would meet for coffee each week, [even] though I didn't know [why] he was discipling me. That was vital. There were so many others at the church who came around me and supported me, recommending books and sermons and praying for me. I would get random ['I'm praying for you today!'] texts all the time. I joined a community group right away. I listened to all of Tim Keller's sermons, as well as John Stott and Dick Lucas. It was a process of people discipling me at my church and God discipling me through these other voices.

During that [time,] right after I got saved, I had a three-month period of no work, which was unusual. [So,] I had all this time to spend with God, to pray and read the Bible. I couldn't stop reading the Bible. Every time I'd listen to a sermon or read the [Bible,] I'd end up in tears: "Oh my gosh, this is true! I can't believe I know God and know the meaning of life finally!"

There are conversations today about whether one can be a "gay Christian." Is there a way to reconcile following Jesus with having a gay identity?

They are irreconcilable. It's strange to me to see these attempts. I had such a clean break from it, and it was entirely God's grace upon me to see that it was necessary. Would you call yourself a greedy Christian? Would you call yourself a tax-collector Christian? It seems strange to identify yourself with sin. It's a square circle. Defining yourself as a "gay Christian," even if you are celibate and not active in a homosexual relationship, is wildly misleading. And it's almost like you're stewing in your old sin, hanging onto your old self in a weird way. It's not helpful to have that moniker over you and to continually identify as such. Why would you identify with your old self that has been crucified with Christ?

[So,] I flee from that term as far as I can. It's not who I am at all. If people ask me how I identify, [I tell them I] don't identify by my sexuality. I'm a follower of Christ who has a lot of struggles, including same-sex attraction." ...

The LGBT movement has gained so much ground by framing homosexuality as an immutable, personhood-level identity. What are your thoughts on the state of how Western culture sees "gay" today?

In the last [twenty] years or [so,] there has been such a huge push to make it sacred. It went from a sin to a sacrament. The book Making Gay Okay does a really good job showing how that happened. Media, movies, TV—it's all been pushing [toward] this. When I was coming of age as a gay kid, it wasn't like this. It was still taboo. There were gay-pride parades, but they weren't at Macy's. Every store in the world didn't have a rainbow on it. But now it's everywhere, it's so dominant, and to say anything against the narrative is seen as crazy if not downright harmful.

Everything is inside out and upside down. The idea of the rainbow, for example, is so odd to me now—using this biblical symbol as the icon of the LGBT movement. When I was gay, I felt shame. Instinctively I knew it was wrong. But though I felt shame, over the [years,] you harden your heart to it. I think the driving force behind these choices, like the rainbow flag and pride parades—the word pride, even—is to convince yourself that there's nothing wrong with it, nothing to be ashamed of. You have to constantly tell yourself that and let the culture tell you that. Because [there's] shame attached to it, so hyper-emphasizing the "rightness" of it helps people embrace their "identity" more.

What is it like watching the "de-conversion" stories of Christians who grow up in the faith but then abandon it because of the LGBT issue? In the [book,] you compare it to Esau selling his birthright for a pot of stew.

I see this happen all the time, especially kids who grew up in Christian families and went to Christian colleges. You can see it coming from a mile away. It's so common, and the culture is so powerful. [I always say look, if you're going to be on social media or Netflix for an hour, you need to read the Bible for an hour because you've just been lied [to,] and now you need the truth.] So yeah, it's very sad.

Your life is a vapor. You're here for two seconds. What do you want your life to be at the [end] when you're on your deathbed? Do you want it to [be that you] got to satisfy all those urges and got the things [you wanted?] Or do you want to be told, [well] done, good and faithful [servant?] You spent your life on mission for the kingdom of [God?]

I often think about Paul, who was single and didn't whine about it. He cared about planting churches and getting the gospel out. He was shipwrecked, beaten, jailed, but he didn't care—he just wanted the gospel out.

To the people who give up, I first and foremost pray, particularly for those I know. It's so sad to me because you're literally giving up your birthright for a single meal. Do you understand what you are doing?

It seems for many Christians who move from holding traditional biblical views on sexuality to being LBGT- "affirming," the thing that moves them over the edge is having someone close to them—a parent, a sibling, a close friend—come out. How should a Christian respond when people close to them come out?

I've seen this happen to several of my friends, and I understand the motivation behind the phenomenon. But the Word of God doesn't change based on our feelings. In terms of responding to those close to us who come out as gay or lesbian, it's important to love them unconditionally without compromising your convictions. As Christians, [we're] in exile. And just as Shadrach and friends refused to bow down to the golden statue in Babylon (Daniel 3), even though the consequences were potentially dire, we have to resist the temptation to bow down to the culture [we're] in —no matter the cost. I'm not saying this is easy.

Some who come out will be super offended when you hold to your traditional biblical views. The issue is now so deeply tied to identity that it can feel like you are rejecting them. I certainly felt that way whenever I remembered that my family, even though they loved me, believed homosexual behavior [was] a sin. Though it wasn't their intent, I felt alienated by them.

[So,] I think the key is to love your friend unconditionally no matter [what] and to pray for them. That's what my sister-in-law did with me. She was an evangelical Christian and knew that I knew what her beliefs were on sexuality (she held the orthodox view). But I never felt an ounce of judgment from her over the years. She just loved me and prayed for me . . . for [twenty] long years. And it worked! The Word of God doesn't change based on our feelings.

... What does change look like for the gay person who becomes a Christian?

When [we're] regenerated, our affections change. Not just in the area of sexuality, but in everything else: our attitude toward money, success, relationships. In terms of so-called conversion therapy, I don't think it's something we should force. I still struggle with same-sex attraction (even though it has greatly diminished and no longer dominates my thought life like it did before God saved me). But he can do anything. He created the universe, so he can reorient our attractions.

Sometimes I pray that God would heal the sexual brokenness in me, especially given that I was molested when I was a child by a friend's father (which I think had a larger effect on my sexual development than I used to admit). Who [knows?] God may change my desires one day. We'll see. But for now, I'm happy to just be single and celibate for the rest of my life. I'm happy to deny myself and take up my cross and follow Jesus.

What have been the biggest costs to you in choosing to follow Jesus? What's been the biggest gain?

God had a lot of grace on me the day he saved me. Giving up the gay life wasn't that difficult; it was actually quite easy. I had just met [Jesus,] and the relationship with him was so overwhelming and wonderful and all-consuming. Oddly enough, I was relieved I didn't have to date anymore.

When you're in that life, you're constantly pressured to date. My friends were always trying to set me up. If you're not in a relationship, people think something's wrong with you. [So,] I was really relieved to not do that anymore. Like I say in the book, all my ex-boyfriends cheated on me, which is common; it's like de rigueur for this world. But in my relationship with [Christ,] I felt so safe. I didn't have to perform.

It was all quid pro quo with my ex-boyfriends. They were all artists. One was in a band that was super successful. One was a major writer in New York. It was always this thing where, if you're not achieving enough or at this certain level, then you might be out. You also had to be in shape all the time! You couldn't be out of shape for two seconds; [otherwise,] you were kicked out of the [club] or had to move to Palm Springs ...

It was such a relief to be in this relationship with Christ. It didn't feel [costly] because I was so full of joy. But it did cost me some friends, some really deep, lifelong relationships. A lot of my friends were semi-supportive, but some of my closest friends were not. That was painful, but at the [time,] I was so euphoric I didn't care.

Once the book came out, some of the friendships that were lingering and semi-alive vanished for good. I was cut off from several people, some of the closest friends of my life. The gain is like Paul said: "I count everything as loss because of the surpassing worth of knowing Christ Jesus my Lord" (Phil. 3:8). Malcolm Muggeridge has that famous quote about how all the fame and money and success of the world is nothing, less than nothing, compared to knowing Christ. The gain is this relationship with God through Christ. Eternal life. It's this impenetrable joy because of not only knowing [Christ] but knowing the meaning of life—where I came from, what I'm doing, where I'm going. It gives me such peace.[158]

THRIVING AFTER INFIDELITY: A STORY OF TWO AFFAIRS

When I was a young girl attending a private Christian school, I knew that there were two reasons for getting a divorce, and no more.

1. Unfaithfulness
2. Abuse of spouse or children

It was presented to me as a set of laws, cut and dry, black and white. I never really thought about it any further than I was told.

I grew up and got married (at the ripe age of 20) and learned immediately that *marriage* is one very hard fight. You're fighting for something you both said you wanted against every ounce of selfishness in each of you combined. For Brian and I, it was very rough and took a long time. We went through loads of hurt and even some betrayal (to a smaller degree than cheating), which I will eventually share, but I finally got it. Marriage is tough, and it's not for the faint of heart. We were willing to stick it out and bury our feet in the dirt, hand-in-hand, but it didn't get any easier until we both matured and let God do some serious work on us.

After seeing how difficult marriage can be, I started thinking about the two laws of marriage I had been taught in school. No wonder it was 'okay' to get a divorce after someone cheats. This thing is hard enough as it is! Who could take that?

Someone who embodies all the humility and grace as Christ Himself did when He walked the soil of [the] earth. Someone who is willing to say no to the hatred wanting to collect in their heart and say yes to the hard road of forgiveness. Someone who knows there's more to life than just being happy, and there's more to [commitment,] too.

Armelina and Ben Stevens were married when they were eighteen and nineteen years [old] in Spring of 2007. They were [Christians] but didn't have relationships with Jesus. Their communication only existed to bring one another [down. They] argued constantly, their lives were all about themselves and never each other.

> "We had no idea what it took to have a good marriage, nor did we care. We each did what we [wanted,]" Armelina tells me.

> "After a few years and three kids, we both ended up having affairs. At that [point,] we were both so broken."

Armelina went on to share with me how her kids were unhappy, aware of their parents' misery, and she and Ben saw that. Ben eventually saw the signs of an affair in his wife, and knowing that he himself had been unfaithful, he went to the pastor who had married them for counsel. The pastor advised him to confess and pray with her, and go from there, which he did.

Some incredible things have happened in the Stevens family since that dark time, and I sat down to interview Armelina and get her story. It's one of those ones that should be shared with the [world] because it's a bright white beam of light and hope in a world where ending a marriage means little more than the inconvenience of paperwork.

Me: [So,] Ben came to you about his affair, knowing about yours, and you sort of had it out that night?

Armelina Stevens: Yes. It was a hard talk to [have,] and I ended up leaving, going outside, and not wanting to talk about it or deal with it for about a week. I was furious with him.

Me: You said divorce was never an option, even after you and your husband came clean about your affairs. What kept you from feeling like your marriage was too broken to be worth saving?

AS: We have always been Christians, but we didn't have a relationship with the Lord. I spent the week after smoking cigarettes outside, processing, thinking of what to do. My husband said he was willing to bring us back to church, get back to God. I saw that God was changing him right before my eyes. I knew that had to mean something good, something different. I just couldn't say 'see ya later' after that. I could see what God was doing and what we were able to become.

Me: What was the state of your feelings toward your husband during your affair? During the reconciliation?

AS: I didn't show much of my negative feelings at first because of the kids. There was this one day where I felt God on me, and my feelings were completely overridden by His presence. I had peace.

After everything happened, I kissed him for the first time in a parking lot, a week after we confessed to each other. That was the most passionate kiss I've ever had. It felt like we were remarried. You could feel the fresh start.

Me: You said your kids were hurting because they saw you were arguing and unhappy together, and you both saw that in them. Did you initially stay together just for them, and [*that's what*] *led into loving each other again?*

AS: It really wasn't about the kids. It was just a desire to be a happily married couple, to love each other through even the toughest times till death do us part. We really wanted that deep down. Our pastor told [us] it's God first, then each other, then your kids. I heard that and thought, [*yes, I want that kind of relationship.*] *Now our kids are so much happier that we are putting each other first.*

Me: You mentioned it took about a week after his confession for your worlds to break down and for you to come together willing to work on things. Why was it a week? What were you [feeling,] and what was going on during that time?

AS: I just felt so guilty for what I had done. I just wanted to cry and get everything out. A part of me wanted to believe that his affair was [worse,] and I was so angry; I wrestled with that during that week. [Eventually,] I realized sin is [sin;] there are no levels. When you ask [forgiveness,] God casts it away from you, and that's it. I knew if things were going to get better, I had to act that out in my marriage.

Me: What would you say to the wife who has been unfaithful and doesn't know what to do now?

AS: Get counseling. Pull your Bible out. Talk to a trustworthy, godly friend who will encourage you in your marriage. I didn't have that. I only had friends who told me to leave my husband. That was so hard, and I had to make friends through a new Bible study. Basically, buckle down and pray. It's so [cliché,] but it's honestly the best thing you can do. That's where God speaks to us.

Me: What would you say to the wife who has been betrayed in her [marriage] and chosen to forgive and move on, but continues to bring up the past to her husband?

AS: [Oh,] I struggled with that so bad for a couple of years after we reconciled. I would just get so angry and irritated, Satan kept reminding me of what Ben had [done,] and I would throw it in his face. The fact is, who was I to say something to him?! I had done the same thing. [So,] to that [wife,] I would say, keep your mouth shut. Open it only to encourage and pray for your heart and for him. You chose to [forgive,] so keep on choosing it.

Me: Were there any specific verses or quotes that really resonated with you during the moving on process?

AS: 1 Corinthians 13:1-13. That's the passage we were given to read together. Love endures all [things;] it never fails. That's God. How amazing is it that we serve a God who forgives and forgets? Not once does God bring it up again. That's a model for us in our marriages. *It's such an overused [passage,] but when I took it for that horrible situation, it came alive and took on a new meaning.*

Me: I'm gonna get awkward and ask the question I think a lot of women need to hear about from someone who has been through it. Was coming together again sexually a bumpy road for the two of you? How soon after everything did that happen for you guys?

AS: It was after we went to counseling. My husband was willing to wait until I was [ready,] and he told me that. I felt God moving us into starting the healing process, and being intimate with one another was what that looked like for us. I didn't need a waiting process.

Me: Do you have any advice for other wives in similar circumstances when it comes to being intimate with their husbands again?

AS: Do it only when you're ready. When you feel completely ready to give yourself back to your husband physically and not think about anyone else, that's the time. Before our [affairs,] we were both bored and just not really trying. After all this happened, our intimacy is amazing. I'm so glad you're asking me about this because it's a part of the process I think is surprising that I really wanted to share to encourage someone who needs to hear this. I wasn't enjoying it before at all, but now sex is so much more pleasurable and romantic and sweet. [We're] so much more connected. [I'm] more attracted to [him,] and I can't wait for him to get home every night. Every time [we're together,] it gets better. [I'm] so thankful for the changes that difficult time brought to our sex life. God woke us up. He woke us up in every area. We weren't having intimacy before.

Me: Do you think that's because you weren't giving yourselves over to each other emotionally that your physical intimacy wasn't satisfying?

AS: Yes, absolutely.

. . .

Ben and Armelina are the pictures of what God can do if you'll allow him into your relationships and into the brokenness that comes from being human. [I'm] so honored they let me share their story and so thankful to Armelina for her raw honesty. We shouldn't feel shameful for our stories of sin and restoration. These are the stories that will change the world.[159]

FREE FROM PEDOPHILIA

Can I be free from Pedophilia? I don't think the sexual feelings will ever go away [on] this side of heaven. [It's] possible that God could do a miracle and rewire a person's brain, and I believe that might happen for some people - God treats us all as individuals. But that's not been the case for me, and the sexual feelings are still there. However, [I'm] free from pedophilia in the sense that it doesn't rule my life.

I used to be held captive by [it] daily. Unwanted thoughts would tumble into my mind, which would lead to fantasies. The step between fantasies and taking action can be a small one. Pornography is one of the first steps toward harming a child. Feeling guilty and ashamed would occupy the rest of my day.

The tension can be overwhelming at times. A friend described it as a faucet that's running, but there's no drain. It threatens to overflow and make a horrible mess. Where can we find help?

Jesus said that he would bring freedom to the prisoners chained in darkness. I so desperately needed his [help] because I couldn't escape on my own. In the Bible, God [led] his people out of slavery in Egypt. He said he [wanted] to do that for all his children. I know [I'm] a slave to pedophilia. It troubled my past, bullies me now, and threatens my future. How can God lead me to freedom? How will Jesus break these chains?

The answer: A new life.

Jesus starts a new life inside you that's different from the old life. That may sound weird, but it makes perfect sense. If I ask Jesus to be part of my life, he brings something new. It begins small, but when I choose to share that new life with him, it gets stronger. Little by little, it overcomes the old.

The new life is a spiritual life. That's where the expression "born again" comes from. It's like being born a second time. It's hard to explain unless you've experienced it, but it's definitely different. It's like seeing new colors – how would you explain it? All you can do is say it's "like" this or that…

It's like hope that you can stand on. It's [believing,] but you can know. It's like being happy, except it's a joy that goes beyond any reason you can find. It's like being loved, and it's a love that makes you greater. It gives you purpose like a fire burning inside. It's being [clean] because you're continually washed from the inside out. [It's] the best experience in all the world to be loved by God and to let him give you his new life!

The choice belongs to you and me every step of the way. God will never force himself on a person. He is very humble. I know that I could choose to walk away at any point. I could tell [him no]. But, where would I go? With [him,] I found love and life.

Each time I choose to follow him, that new life gets stronger. I don't look at inappropriate material. I turn my [head] rather than stare. I don't allow my mind to fantasize. I have strict boundaries with children. Feelings of attraction may come, but they don't occupy my thoughts or rule my daily life. God has led me down a path of freedom from pedophilia.

I recognize that these are behavior choices, and someone will say that I'm curing myself without any help from God. I don't believe that's [true] because I know from personal experience that my own willpower was never enough to sidestep sexual attraction. If God is real (and I believe he is), a relationship with him must have profound effects. [We, humans,] are influenced by the company we keep, and I recommend anyone [to] spend time in the company of Jesus. It will change you.

When God looks at you, he sees you as a new creation in Christ. You have a new identity that was created when Jesus rose from the grave. You are in the process of living that out – "growing in every way more and more like Christ" (Eph 4:15). Yes, those feelings of attraction remain; pedophilia is a physical condition that affects our neurons. [But,] you are now a child of God, and you are walking step by step forward with him.

Pedophilia gave me shame, isolation, and the risk of harming others. God has given me love, healthy relationships, and the freedom to live again. I know that pedophilia will present a challenge until I go to [heaven;] therefore, I guard myself. [But] I'm not in chains anymore. Jesus set me free.

> (Jesus) found the place where it is written: The Spirit of the Lord is on me, because he has anointed me to proclaim good news to the poor. He has sent me to proclaim freedom for the prisoners and recovery of sight for the blind, to set the oppressed free, to proclaim the year of the Lord's favor. And He closed the book, gave it back to the attendant and sat down; and the eyes of all in the synagogue were fixed on Him. And He began to say to them, 'Today this Scripture has been fulfilled in your hearing.' ~Luke 4:16-21

> "Come to me, all you who are weary and burdened, and I will give you rest. Take my yoke upon you and learn from me, for I am gentle and humble in heart, and you will find rest for your souls. For my yoke is easy and my burden is light." ~Matthew 28:29-30[160]

I WAS A PROSTITUTE, BUT JESUS TOLD ME I BELONG TO HIM FOREVER

In the autumn, Jaleh, a quiet, rather sullen woman, arrived at an Elam conference. Nobody knew that when she was [fourteen,] she had been raped as a punishment for joining a school protest; that when she told the authorities they had whipped her for immorality; that her father had then repeatedly abused her; as did other relatives. Nobody knew shame had driven Jaleh to the streets to work as a prostitute, nor of all the babies aborted from her womb. All that was known was that she had recently become a Christian through a house church and had a husband who was scornful [toward] her new faith. At the end of the conference, apart from one leader, this woman's past was still private. But what everyone knew, just from her face, was that she had had an encounter with Jesus Christ. Here Jaleh tells her story:

A few months after I became a [Christian,] I went to a conference just for women. Their stories encouraged me, but I started to worry about why He never spoke to [me] or came into my dreams. I decided they were better than me. I was not worthy enough for Him to get near to me. Until [now,] my past was a complete secret, but I decided to share [it] with one of the ladies leading the conference.

I told her everything and then asked for a glimpse of Jesus in my dream. The lady did not promise a [dream] but kept on reassuring me of God's love for me. For the next few [nights,] I slept, expecting to see Jesus. He did not come. I thought that it was because of my past. I was not good enough. A painful darkness grew inside me, and [even during this] conference, I thought of running away and going back to prostitution.

[Again,] I went to the leader and asked for prayer to dream about Jesus. She was happy to [pray] but was firm about the dream. "You cannot box God in. [It's] up to Him how He reveals Himself to you." We prayed and [prayed,] and I got bored. I really wanted her to finish so I could go to bed and maybe dream of Jesus.

But as we prayed, I softened. I began to feel God's presence and His presence was thicker and [thicker] until I could not stand up [anymore]. I was frightened with a Holy fear. I kept [screaming: '[I'm] frightened! Do something! He is awesome…help me. [I'm] frightened!'] But I could not come out of His presence.

The lady told me not to be frightened and to enjoy His presence. Oh, I was so full of praise! His presence was wonderful. I wanted to stay there [forever] and praise Him. I could not find words for the adoration I felt. A jumble of songs came out!

It was as if my whole being was rejoicing and dancing before Him. I could not see His [face,] but He was there looking at me. He said, "Were you about to give up? Did you know that [I'm] your friend? I love you! I love you! I have always loved you. You are mine!" His hands were so strong. He held my [hands,] and it was as if we were dancing together. I felt that my body was light and lifted to Him. I was free from any burden of guilt and shame; I was light as a feather. I was so full of joy that I remember I started laughing uncontrollably. I felt that Jesus was laughing with me. I was swirling and laughing and praising. I felt that the sky was opening and that a shiny light came down surrounding me.

When I went home after the conference, my husband could not believe the changes in me. I told him about my encounter with Jesus. He asked me to pray for him. He started coming to church with [me,] and now he has become a Christian. I was a [prostitute,] but as He told me in my vision, [I'm] His; I belong to Him [forever,] and nothing can take this away from me.

Modern Day Magdalene

Jaleh's story doesn't stop with her salvation. Like Mary Magdalene in the Bible, her [life] and her family's life has been truly transformed by the grace and love of Jesus Christ. She, [along] with her husband (who is now clean of drugs), are now committed members of a house church where they are growing as Christians. Life for them is [hard.] Jaleh's husband works as a market trader in a notorious part of town where drug dealers and prostitutes congregate. This presents much opportunity to evangelize but also temptations from the past are never far away. They feel called to life in full-time [ministry, and] so are praying that if [it's] God's will that they will have an opportunity to study.[161]

After introducing these articles, one of the thoughts that came [to mind] was that maybe I shouldn't have introduced as many. And then I thought, why, as a reader should we be in a hurry. This book is all about helping others not only in their dysfunctional sexual relationships but also in every aspect of their lives. Hopefully, one or more of these stories will have impacted someone who is reading this book and provide them with the insight needed to either make a decision for God to come into their life and make them a new person or if God has already done so to apply some of the insights that will help them learn how to become a daily overcomer in whatever area of sexual inclinations that have had a hold over them.

As many have said in these articles that in order to change within, you need someone who can provide the changes needed. The initial change that is needed is to receive a new nature. Only God can give you this. Would you like to receive this new nature right now? If you would, then say these words inwardly or out loud.

God the Father, I acknowledge that I have sinned in many areas, such as slandering others; having sexual relations outside of marriage; being jealous; having participated in alcohol or drug abuse; having sex with others of the same gender; committing adultery; taking money from others in a deceitful manner; committed rape; engaged in pedophilia; etc. I don't want to continue in these mental, verbal, and overt sins. I need a new nature.

I believe in your Son Jesus Christ as one of the members of the Trinity, who as God pre-existed time; came to the earth and took on the form of a man, being born of a virgin (no sin nature); lived a sinless life; listened to and obeyed the directives of his Father; went to the cross and paid for the penalty of and forgave the sins of the whole world; rose from the dead after three days, never to die again, walked the earth in His resurrection body for forty days witnessing to over five hundred people, and ascended into heaven to be seated at the right hand of God the Father.

And according to your promise, send the Holy Spirit to come and indwell my body thus imparting to me a new nature. Thank you, I'm now a new spiritual creature. Now, begin to assist me in helping me to overcome whatever areas are in my life that have brought about misery so that I can learn how to be set free from them. Again, thank you.

I have one last section to leave you with. Contained are my closing thoughts. I'll see you there.

EPILOGUE

FULFILLING MY SPIRITUAL DESTINY

I hope you enjoyed this study. I can only say I had no idea of writing on the topic of *TESTIMONY*. Certain events seemed to take place, which drew me to this subject, such as reporting about the sexual abuse of young boys in a mainstream church on TV and an article about a different mainstream church that my wife found online whose founder confessed to having engaged in such. And so, I decided to read this article in which some of the members of this church had expressed their sexual preferences for members of the same sex and felt that they were unjustly treated by fellow believers and church leaders.

So, after hearing their comments, I decided to see if what they said their concerns were, was supported by Scripture. This was done not to condemn them but to provide scriptural clarity, whether in agreement with their comments or not. All of us, Christians, have perceptions about this or that to which only the Word of God can provide the answers. Once we know what the Word has to say, then it's up to us to obey its instructions or not.

One who can testify that walking by faith is not easy is me. After I got saved and began to hear sound doctrinal teaching, I soon realized how most of my thoughts, words, and actions were not aligned with how God would have me to think, speak, and act. Some beautiful descriptions of what the words *sound doctrine* mean are found in the book of 2 Timothy.

2 Timothy 4:3

> *For the time will come when they will not endure sound doctrine; but after their own lusts shall they heap to themselves teachers, having itching ears;*

The words *sound doctrine* refers to sound (or healthful) doctrine, with reference to the effect produced because it actually instructs to godliness.[162] Another definition for *sound doctrine* is that it's doctrine contributing to the health of the soul.[163] As I continued to hear about how God thought about me, I decided to appropriate these truths for myself, and subsequently, the realization of God's perspective slowly became the reality of how I thought about myself, others, and the circumstances of life. There's a beautiful verse that exemplifies this.

Galatians 6:8

> *For he that soweth to his flesh shall of the flesh reap corruption; but he that soweth to the Spirit shall of the Spirit reap life everlasting.*

He that chooses to sow (to concentrate on) the natural desires of his flesh will reap corruption (moral and spiritual decay). But he that chooses to sow (to concentrate on) the desires of the Spirit, i.e., the desire of promoting his own spiritual growth[164] and of concentrating on the fruit of the Spirit[165] will reap life everlasting. What does it mean to reap life everlasting? It means we reap the blessings of the eternal life which God has given him.[166] And just what are these blessings of eternal life that God has given us? Some of these blessings are found in the book of 1 John.

1 John 5:11

> *And this is the record, that God hath given to us eternal life, and this life is in his Son.*

The words *eternal life* refers to the *zoe* or abundant life that God has given us. The *zoe* life pertains to all those superadded things which are needful to make that life eminently blessed and happy.[167] Some of these superadded things are the indwelling Holy Spirit and His fruit (influences; graces; elements of character), which when developed causes us to have rest [(refreshment and rejuvenation) for our souls; to experience times of refreshing (divine peace regulating, ruling, and harmonizing the heart) and joy (inner happiness without any kind of mental agony or fear); and to operate in righteousness (correctness in thinking, feeling and acting; upright character and disposition; integrity)].

Is this the kind of life you want to operate in?

If you do, then choose to sow to the Word of God and the Spirit, and you will see the sexual inclinations, passions, and desires of your flesh decrease and all that God has for you to operate in increase so that your life evidences these inner changes to both believers and unbelievers, who will be drawn to want to find out how your life has been so dramatically transformed.

God Bless You!

If you would like to communicate with me, then please respond via my email address: rondolord@hotmail.com. My website is www.makingtheonerightchoice.com. I also provide weekly teachings on various biblical topics by following this link: http://bit.ly/1N9SHdX.

ENDNOTES

[1]Brandy Zadrozny. "Sex Abuse & Gay Conversion Therapy: The Dark Past of Justin Bieber's Megachurch Hillsong," 2016. 01 January 2019

<https://bit.ly/3j6fdh2>.

[2] Sex Abuse & Gay Conversion Therapy.

[3] Sex Abuse & Gay Conversion Therapy.

[4] Sex Abuse & Gay Conversion Therapy.

[5] Sex Abuse & Gay Conversion Therapy.

[6] Sex Abuse & Gay Conversion Therapy.

[7] *Barnes' Notes. Pc Study Bible version 5, 2006.* BIBLESOFT. WEB. 01 January 2019

<http://www.biblesoft.com>.

[8] *The Pulpit Commentary Pc Study Bible version 5, 2006.* BIBLESOFT. WEB. 03 January 2019

<http://www.biblesoft.com>.

[9]*Weust Word Studies from the Greek New Testament Pc Study Bible version 5, 2005.* BIBLESOFT. WEB. 06 January 2019

<http://www.biblesoft.com>.

[10] Sex Abuse & Gay Conversion Therapy.

[11] Sex Abuse & Gay Conversion Therapy.

[12] Weust.

[13] Weust.

[14] Barnes.

[15]*The Bible Exposition Commentary/New Testament 1989.* BIBLESOFT. WEB. 10 January 2019 <http://www.biblesoft.com>.

[16]The Bible Exposition Commentary/New Testament.

[17]*Adam Clarke's Commentary Pc Study Bible version 5, 2004.* BIBLESOFT. WEB. 15 January 2019 <http://www.biblesoft.com>.

[18] *IVP Bible Background Commentary Pc Study Bible version 5, 2005.* BIBLESOFT. WEB. 20 January 2019 <http://www.biblesoft.com>.

[19]*UBS New Testament Handbook Series Pc Study Bible version 5, 2005.* BIBLESOFT. WEB. 25 January 2019 <http://www.biblesoft.com>.

[20] Adam Clarke's Commentary.

[21] Adam Clarke's Commentary.

[22] The Bible Exposition Commentary/New Testament.

[23] Barnes.

[24] The Pulpit Commentary.

[25] UBS.

[26]The Bible Exposition Commentary/New Testament.

[27] *Thayer's Greek Lexicon Pc Study Bible version 5, 2006.* BIBLESOFT. WEB. 01 February 2019 <http://www.biblesoft.com>.

[28] UBS.

[29] *Greek-English Lexicon Pc Study Bible version 5, 2005.* BIBLESOFT. WEB. 10 February 2019 <http://www.biblesoft.com>.

[30] *Robertson's New Testament Word Pictures Pc Study Bible version 5, 2005.* BIBLESOFT. WEB. 15 February 2019 <http://www.biblesoft.com>.

[31] Robertson.

[32]Bible Knowledge Commentary/New Testament.

[33] Dictionary.com.

[34] Barnes.

[35] The Pulpit Commentary.

[36] Sex Abuse & Gay Conversion Therapy.

[37] Weust.

[38] Robertson.

[39] The Bible Exposition Commentary/New Testament.

[40]The Bible Exposition Commentary/New Testament.

[41] Sex Abuse & Gay Conversion Therapy.

[42] Sex Abuse & Gay Conversion Therapy.

[43] Weust.

[44] Thayer's Greek Lexicon.

[45] Adam Clarke's Commentary.

[46] Weust.

[47] *Jamieson, Faucet, and Brown Commentary Pc Study Bible version 5, 2005*. BIBLESOFT. WEB. 27 February 2019
<http://www.biblesoft.com>.

[48] Adam Clarke's Commentary.

[49] Weust.

[50] Adam Clarke's Commentary.

[51]Bible Knowledge Commentary/New Testament.

[52]The Bible Exposition Commentary/New Testament.

[53] Barnes.

[54] Weust.

[55] Dictionary.com.

[56] Weust.

[57] The Pulpit Commentary.

[58] Weust.

[59] Adam Clarke's Commentary.

[60]Jamieson, Faucet, and Brown Commentary.

[61] "Four Greek Words for "Love","
<https://bit.ly/3aqh50w>.

[62] Barnes.

[63] Dictionary.com.

[64] Weust.

[65] Weust.

[66] Dictionary.com.

[67] Jamieson, Faucet, and Brown.

[68] Four Greek Words for "Love".

[69] Weust.

[70]Jamieson, Faucet, and Brown Commentary.

[71]The Bible Exposition Commentary/New Testament.

[72] The Pulpit Commentary.

[73]Weust.

[74]*Calvin's Commentaries. Pc Study Bible version 5, 2006.* BIBLESOFT. WEB. 20 March 2019
<http://www.biblesoft.com>.

[75] Four Greek Words for "Love".

[76]Tim Challies, "Roman Sexuality Was About Dominance," <https://bit.ly/2YveZKq>.

[77]Timothy Williams, "Why a Vote on Gay Clergy and Same-Sex Marriage Could Split the United Methodist Church," 2019.
<https://nyti.ms/3AkRNLT>.

[78]Nicole Alcindor. "EVANGELICALS PUSH FOR NEW BISHOP AFTER CHURCH IN WALES ALLOWS PASTORS TO BLESS GAY MARRIAGES," *THE CHRISTIAN POST.* 30 September 2021
<https://bit.ly/2WrnxRF>.

[79] Barnes.

[80] Robertson's New Testament.

[81] Weust.

[82] Jamieson, Faucet, and Brown.

[83]The Bible Exposition Commentary/New Testament.

[84]Bible Knowledge Commentary/New Testament.

[85] Adam Clarke's Commentary.

[86] Adam Clarke's Commentary.

[87] Barnes.

[88] IVP Bible Background Commentary.

[89]*UBS Old Testament Handbook Series Pc Study Bible version 5, 2005.* BIBLESOFT. WEB. 01 April 2019
<http://www.biblesoft.com>.

[90]"Laws regarding incest,"
<https://bit.ly/3AnIYBe>.

[91] UBS New Testament.

[92] UBS New Testament.

[93] Adam Clarke's Commentary.

[94] Calvin's Commentaries.

[95] Robertson's New Testament.

[96] Dictionary.com.

[97] "JOSEPH - Male sexual abuse survivor," <https://bit.ly/3v2M50o>.

[98] Sex Abuse & Gay Conversion Therapy.

[99] Adam Clarke's Commentary.

[100] The Pulpit Commentary.

[101] American Dictionary of the English Language. 6 October 2021 <http://www.webstersdictionary1828.com>.

[102] *Bible Exposition Commentary/Old Testament, 2004.* BIBLESOFT. WEB. 2 October 2021 <http://www.biblesoft.com>.

[103] Jamieson, Faucet, and Brown Commentary.

[104] Barnes.

[105] Adam Clarke's Commentary.

[106] Adam Clarke's Commentary.

[107] Barnes.

[108] Weust.

[109] Barnes.

[110] Weust.

[111] Barnes.

[112] Sex Abuse & Gay Conversion Therapy.

[113] UBS New Testament.

[114] Weust.

[115] UBS New Testament.

[116] Barnes.

[117] Barnes.

[118] Jamieson, Faucet, and Brown Commentary.

[119] UBS New Testament.

[120] Weust.

[121] UBS New Testament.

[122] IVP Bible Background Commentary.

[123] UBS New Testament.

[124] Adam Clarke's Commentary.

[125] Weust.

[126] *Thayer's Greek Lexicon and Brown Driver & Briggs Hebrew Lexicon Pc Study Bible version 5, 2005.* BIBLESOFT. WEB. 11 April 2019 <http://www.biblesoft.com>.

[127] Jamieson, Faucet, and Brown Commentary.

[128] The Bible Exposition Commentary/New Testament.

[129] Robertson.

[130] UBS New Testament.

[131] *A Greek-English Lexicon of the New Testament: Being Grimm's Wilke's Clavis* <https://books.google.com/books?id=1E4VAAAAYAAJ>.

[132] Thayer's Greek Lexicon and Brown Driver & Briggs Hebrew Lexicon.

[133] *Vincent's New Testament Word Studies Pc Study Bible version 5, 2005.* 16 April 2019 <http://www.biblesoft.com>.

[134] Jamieson, Faucet, and Brown Commentary.

[135] Weust.

[136] Weust.

[137] The Bible Exposition Commentary/New Testament.

[138] Barnes.

[139] Weust.

[140] The Bible Exposition Commentary/New Testament.

[141] Calvin's Commentaries.

[142] The Pulpit Commentary.

[143] Adam Clarke's Commentary.

[144] UBS New Testament.

[145] Thayer's Greek Lexicon and Brown Driver & Briggs Hebrew

Lexicon.

[146] Jamieson, Faucet, and Brown Commentary.

[147] UBS New Testament.

[148] Weust.

[149] Weust.

[150] Weust.

[151] Dictionary.com.

[152] Adam Clarke's Commentary.

[153] Adam Clarke's Commentary.

[154] Barnes.

[155] UBS New Testament.

[156] Weust.

[157] Kayla Armstrong, "Joyce Meyer overcame abuse by her father," 2017. *GODREPORTS*. 15 January, 2020 <https://bit.ly/3ApIzhq>.

[158] Becket Cook and Brett McCracken, "From Gay to Gospel: The Fascinating Story of Becket Cook," 2019. TGC. 17 January 2020 <https://bit.ly/2YCCEsD>.

[159] Allie Casazza, "Thriving After Infidelity: A Story of Two Affairs,"2016. <https://alliecasazza.com/blog/happy-marriage-after-affair-infidelity/>.

[160] "Free from Pedophilia," 14 January 2020 <https://bit.ly/2YwX9ai>.

[161] "I was a prostitute, but Jesus told me I belong to Him forever," *Elam.* 15 January 2020 <https://bit.ly/3lqgX7I>.

[162] Calvin's Commentaries.

[163] Barnes.

[164] *Bible Knowledge Commentary/ Old Testament, 2000.* 20 April 2019 <http://www.biblesoft.com>.

[165] UBS New Testament.

[166] Weust.

[167] Barnes.

Made in United States
North Haven, CT
10 June 2022

20103002R00083